ALEXANDER POPE

THE POET AND THE LANDSCAPE

ALEXANDER POPE

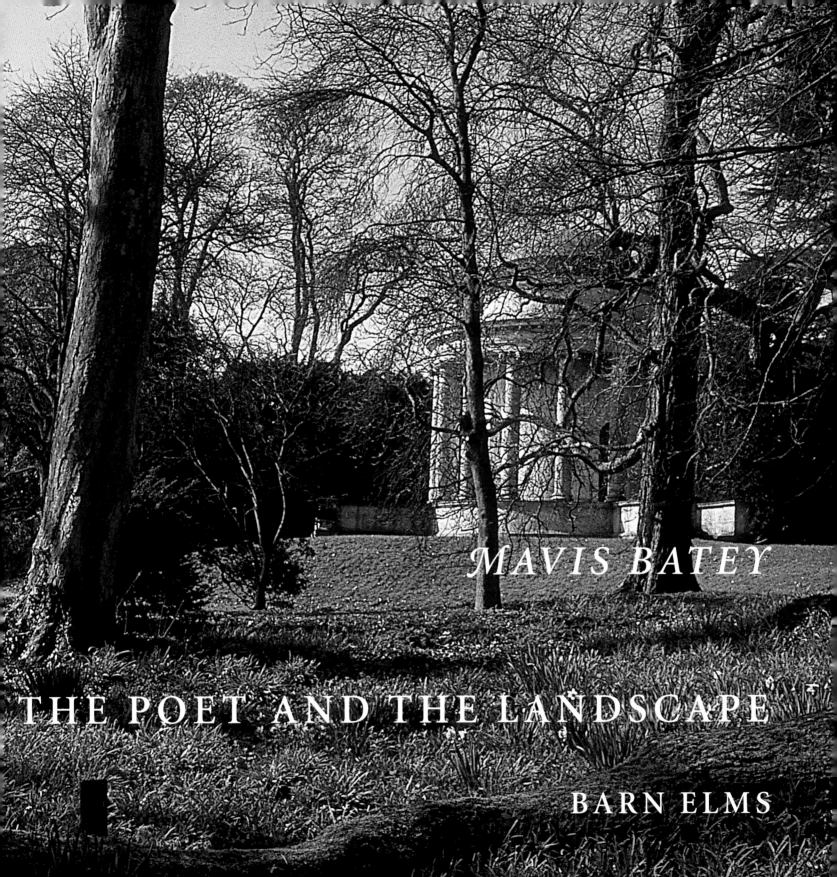

MAVIS BATEY

THE POET AND THE LANDSCAPE

BARN ELMS

This book is dedicated to Kim Wilkie, author of the Thames Landscape Strategy, for whom Pope's vision of man's relationship with place is the inspiration of his landscape design practice.

Published in 1999 by Barn Elms Publishing
93 Castelnau, London SW13 9EL

Printed in Hong Kong by Midas Printing Ltd. Set in Minion.
All rights reserved.

Text copyright © 1999 Mavis Batey

Designed by Jessica Smith

Mavis Batey has asserted her right to be identified
as the author of this work.

British Library Cataloguing in Publication Data. A catalogue record of this book
is available from the British Library.

ISBN 1 899531 05 X

Title-page. The Elysian Fields at Stowe.
It was in the landscape garden at Stowe that the art which brought
poetry, painting and gardening together was first displayed.

CONTENTS

CHRONOLOGY

Chiswick Villa was the centre of the arts in Augustan England. It was Lord Burlington who brought Pope the poet and Kent the painter together, an introduction which would lead to the new art of landscape gardening.

1688   Alexander Pope born in London, 21 May.

1700   Pope family moves to Binfield in Windsor Forest.

1709   Pope's *Pastorals* published in Tonson's *Miscellany*.

1711   Shaftesbury's *Characteristicks*: neoclassical ideas; linked aesthetics and morals and ushered in the Man of Taste. Burlington took up his call to establish a national taste.

1711   Pope's *Essay on Criticism* setting out the principles of taste and the authority of the ancients; praised by Addison.

1712   Addison's 'Pleasures of the Imagination' essays in *The Spectator* extended Locke's 'new way of ideas' to aesthetics.

1712   Pope becomes acquainted with Swift, Gay, Parnell and Arbuthnot, who form the Scriblerus Club.

1713   Pope begins to take lessons in painting from Jervas

1713   Pope's *Guardian* essay advocating the 'amiable Simplicity of unadorned Nature' as the 'Taste of the Ancients'.

1713   Pope's 'Windsor Forest' published; 'locus amoenus' of pastoral poetry with its forest lawns, opening glades and flowery meadows, which Spence said was akin to his later thoughts on gardening.

1713   Pope attends Whiston's astronomy lectures at Addison's London coffee house.

1715   Pope becomes acquainted with Lady Mary Wortley Montagu.

1715   Switzer's *The Nobleman, Gentleman and Gardener's Recreation* quotes 'Windsor Forest' as 'a true forest landskip' and proposes 'rural and extensive gardening'. He adapts Pope's general classical precepts to gardening.

1715   First volume of Pope's translation of Homer's *Iliad* published.

1715   First volume of Colen Campbell's *Vitruvius Britannicus* published.

1716   Pope's family leaves Binfield and settles 'under the Wing of my Lord Burlington' at Mawsons New Buildings, Chiswick.

1717   Pope's father dies.

1719   Death of Addison.

1719   Pope begins building his Twickenham villa.

1719   Princess Caroline calls a gardening conference at Richmond to which Pope is invited.

1719   Burlington returns from second Grand Tour with Kent.

1719   Pope pays court to Henrietta Howard, the Chloe of his Eclogues, at Richmond.

1720   *The Iliad* finished. Gay's 'Mr Pope's Welcome from Greece' published.

1720   Kent illustrates Gay's *Poems on Several Occasions*.

1725   Pope's *Odyssey* illustrated by William Kent.

1725   Bolingbroke returns from exile and settles near Pope.

1726   Voltaire visits Pope.

1726   Pope visited by Swift. *Gulliver's Travels* published.

1726   Joseph Spence meets Pope after publishing 'An Essay on Pope's Odyssey' and remains a friend for the rest of his life, attending him in his final illness.

1726-30   Thomson's *The Seasons*.

1727   Swift's second visit to Pope.

1727   Kent illustrates Gay's *Fables*.

1727   George I dies.

1728   *The Dunciad* published in three books.

1728   Batty Langley's *New Principles of Gardening*.

1728   Robert Castell's *Villas of the Ancients Illustrated*.

1728   Gay's *The Beggar's Opera*.

1730   Kent illustrates Thomson's *The Seasons*.

1731   Pope's important *Epistle to the Earl of Burlington*.

1732   Gilbert West's poem on Stowe dedicated to Pope.

1732   Kent's first garden, for the Prince of Wales, at Carlton House.

1733   Pope's mother dies.

1735   Curll's edition of Pope's letters.

1737   Queen Caroline dies.

1738   Bolingbroke stays with Pope while he sells Dawley; discusses his idea for 'a Patriot King' with him.

1738   Kent works at Rousham.

1739   Pope visits Rousham after Stowe.

1739   Prince of Wales sends urns to Pope for his garden.

1740   Pope visits Bath and Avon Gorge; stays with Ralph Allen and sees the Bath stone mines, which influence his 'grottofying'.

1744   Death of Pope, 30 May.

LIST OF ILLUSTRATIONS

INTRODUCTION

Rousham, Oxfordshire. The English natural style garden
had strong literary and philosophical origins. Pope's influence
on Kent is nowhere more apparent than in the
'practical poetry' of Venus Vale.

Alexander Pope (1688-1744), the foremost poet of his age. He is seen here aged about twenty eight in a portrait by Jonathan Richardson with his Great Dane, Bounce. Bounce's puppies were given to fellow gardeners; they roamed the landscape gardens of Stowe, Hagley, Kew, Prior Park, Wimpole and Cirencester.

'national taste' that Shaftesbury had called for. By the 1730s Pope's poetic sensibility to landscape and the ideas of 'Kent the painter' combined to establish the 'national taste' in gardening, acclaimed throughout the world as 'the English garden'.

Pope's famous maxim, 'Consult the Genius of the Place in All', instanced as 'Good Sense' in his *Epistle to the Earl of Burlington*, would provide a sound basis for future environmental planning. The ideas still manifest at Chiswick, Stowe and Rousham would lead on to the Picturesque movement and its lasting legacy of visual appreciation, to the public parks movement and its provision for the spiritual refreshment of city dwellers, to town and country planning, to professional landscape architecture and to the strength of the amenity movement in this country.

The Great Room in the Greenwich Observatory, *c.* 1675. 'First follow Nature', but in Newton's age 'Nature's works' were related to cosmology rather than scenery.

1. 'Summer: the Second Pastoral, or Alexis', ll.59-60.
2. G. de Beer and A.M.Rousseau, 'Voltaire's British Visitors', in *Studies on Voltaire*, XLix (1967), p.75.
3. 'Epitaph XII: Intended for Sir Isaac Newton, in Westminster Abbey'.
4. Richard Hurd, *Letters on Chivalry and Romance*, 1762, Letter 1, p.2.
5. Shaftesbury (Anthony Ashley Cooper), *The Moralists*, 1709, in *Characteristics*, ed. J.M.Robertson, 1964, III, ii, p.125.
6. *The Correspondence of Alexander Pope*, ed. George.Sherburn, 5 vols, 1956, 2:14.

'TAKE NATURE'S PATH'

A scene in Windsor Forest painted by Paul Sandby. Pope
derived his ideas on natural gardening from Windsor Forest,
where, as a youth, he rode daily.

See what Delights in Sylvan Scenes appear!
Descending Gods have found Elysium here.
In Woods bright Venus with Adonis stray'd,
And chaste Diana haunts the Forest Shade.
Come lovely Nymph, and bless the silent Hours,
When Swains from Sheering seek their nightly Bow'rs;
When weary Reapers quit the sultry Field,
And crown'd with Corn, their Thanks to Ceres yield.
This harmless Grove no lurking Viper hides,
But in my Breast the Serpent Love abides
Here bees from Blossoms sip the rosie Dew,
But your Alexis knows no Sweets but you.
Oh deign to visit our forsaken Seats,
The mossie Fountains, and the Green Retreats!
Where-e'er you walk, cool Gales shall fan the Glade,
Trees, where you sit, shall crowd into a Shade,
Where-e'er you tread, the blushing Flow'rs shall rise,
And all things flourish where you turn your Eyes.

Alexander Pope, *Pastorals, Summer, The Second Pastoral,*
or Alexis, 1709, lines 59–76.

The *Pastorals* were headed with the following lines from Virgil:

Rura mihi & rigui placeant in vallibus amnes,
Flumina amem, sylvasque, inglorius!

Alexander Pope's early years at Binfield on the edge of Windsor Forest were ideal for the making of a poet, philosopher and advocate of natural gardening. He went to live there at the age of twelve when his father, a successful linen draper, retired from the City. Pope had no more formal education but lived a life where his fancy led him, 'like a Boy gathering flowers', walking in the woods or along the river and reading extensively in his father's library and those of the neighbouring gentry.[1]

Pope's first verse, written when he was sixteen and published in Tonson's *Miscellany* in 1709, was in the time-honoured pastoral strain. In an introductory essay Pope defined the pastoral as 'an image of the Golden Age'. The originator of pastoral poetry, Theocritus, described in his bucolic idylls the simple life of the Sicilian shepherd following his flocks. Virgil, in his *Eclogues*, looked back on this far-away world as a golden age and Pope tried to emulate it in his own modern times. 'Feed here my lambs, I'll seek no distant field', he wrote as a 'musing shepherd'. The sweetness and simplicity of Pope's pastoral, where Alexis, the Virgilian shepherd boy, lived in tune with nature, was perfectly captured by Handel when he put lines from Pope's 'Summer' to music in *Semele*:

> *Where-e'er you walk, cool Gales shall fan the Glade,*
> *Trees, where you sit, shall crowd into a Shade.*

Whilst still in his youth, Pope had the first of several illnesses which left him with ruined health and a tubercular spine affliction which eventually deformed him. In 1705, at the age of seventeen, when he might have made the Grand Tour to complete his classical studies, he had a much more severe attack and resigned himself to death, writing round to his friends in great distress. Thomas Southcote, a fellow Roman Catholic, was well acquainted with Oxford's great Dr Radcliffe and asked his advice; less study and daily rides in the forest were prescribed. The young Pope set about striking a balance in his 'perpetual application' and was soon able to return to his intensive reading and writing and take long rides for exercise, immersed in classical reverie.

A constant companion on these rides in the forest was Sir William Trumbull, a former Secretary of State, from neighbouring Easthampstead Park. He was a great lover of the classics and encouraged Pope to think about translating Homer. Pope was particularly inspired by the 'imaging' parts of Homer and by Virgil's poetry, which, like Addison, he felt 'raises in our minds a pleasing variety of scenes and landscapes'.[2] Addison sought out the actual landscapes described by Virgil, but Pope, whose frailty prevented him from making the Grand Tour, had to transfer the imagery of 'classic ground' to 'blest Thames's shores'. This intensified his poetic sensitivity to his surroundings so that even when confined indoors in inclement weather he could write, 'I am endeavouring to raise up around me a painted scene of woods and forests in verdure and beauty…I am wandering through bowers and grottoes in conceit'.[3]

Soon he had a true companion in Martha Blount, who could fulfil the role of shepherdess in the shades of Windsor Forest. Martha and her sister Teresa, whom he found charming with their 'endless smiles', lived by the Thames at Mapledurham near Reading. Pope probably met them at Whiteknights, the home of their grandfather, Sir Anthony Englefield, said to be a 'lover of poetry and poets'.[4] Pope presented the two sisters with a copy of 'The Rape of the Lock' in 1712, and in 1717 when he had left Binfield he composed a nostalgic poem for them, remembering his early days and the visionary scenes in Windsor Forest in which they had played a part:

> *All hail! Once pleasing, once inspiring Shade,*
> *Scene of my youthful Loves, and happier hours!*
> *Where the kind Muses met me as I stray'd*
> *And gently pressed my hand, and said, Be Ours.*[5]

It soon became apparent, however, that it was 'blue-eyed' Martha, with her 'Romantick taste', who was the

Charles Jervas's painting of Martha and Teresa Blount. The sisters fulfilled the role of latterday shepherdesses in Pope's pastoral reveries in Windsor Forest: 'Your Alexis knows no Sweets but you'.

poet's real inspiration and soul mate. She would share his thoughts all her life and it is in letters to her, conjuring up 'ideas', that Pope's sensibility to landscape is best expressed.

Pope's friend, Joseph Spence, who was Professor of Poetry at Oxford, said that the sensitive ideas Pope expressed in his pastoral poem 'Windsor Forest', with its green retreats, waving groves, forest lawns, opening glades and flowery meadows, were later akin to his thoughts on gardening.[6] The lines from the poem most frequently quoted by garden commentators were:

> Where order in Variety we see
> And where, tho' all things differ, all agree.

The title-page from Seeley's 1744 guidebook to Stowe quoting Pope's 'Order in Variety'. Guidebooks and commentators frequently quoted from Pope's 'Windsor Forest' with its 'green retreats' when describing landscape gardens.

They were inserted on the title-page of Seeley's *A Description of the Gardens of Lord Viscount Cobham at Stow in Buckinghamshire*, the first comprehensive guide to the gardens of a country seat.

Pope enjoyed working in the Binfield forest garden 'planted by a father's hand'.[7] At the beginning of an article he wrote for *The Guardian* in 1713 he said it had been admired by a man of polite taste.[8] This article, published the same year as 'Windsor Forest', was the poet's first attempt at a garden philosophy. He extolled the 'amiable Simplicity of unadorned Nature', which he had come to appreciate in Windsor Forest through the Arcadian pastoral tradition. He set out, tentatively, to prove that simplicity was 'the Taste of the Ancients in their Gardens' and decried 'Fantastical Operations of Art', particularly trees cut into shapes, as Addison had also done in his articles in *The Spectator* the previous year, when he had called, more explicitly, for a more natural kind of gardening which would extend to the whole estate.[9]

Stephen Switzer was the first professional gardener to heed the remarks of Addison and Pope in his *The Nobleman, Gentleman and Gardener's Recreation*, published in 1715. It broke away from the type of squared formal garden seen in Kip engravings (see page 32) to propose a theory of garden design which would embrace the whole estate. He acknowledged his indebtedness to Addison and quoted Pope's poetic ideas in 'Windsor Forest' as giving the right ideas about 'a true forest landskip'. Switzer advocated 'rural or extensive gardening' and the type of 'forest gardening' practised at Cirencester, which Pope visited in 1718 when he became a close friend of Lord Bathurst and collaborated in his ideas for the park. 'Who plants like Bathurst', he would later say in his *Epistle to the Earl of Burlington*.

Switzer's book had come at an auspicious moment to encourage the peaceful pursuit of gardening. The

A
DESCRIPTION
OF THE
GARDENS
OF
Lord Viſcount COBHAM,
AT
STOW in BUCKINGHAMSHIRE.

Here Order in Variety you ſee,
Where all Things differ, ---- yet where all agree !
A. POPE.

NORTHAMPTON:
Printed by W. DICEY; and ſold by B. *Seeley*, Writing-Maſter, in *Buckingham*, and *George Norris*, Peruke-Maker, in *Newport-Pagnell*, Bucks. M.DCC.XLIV.

Marlborough Wars were over and many returning noblemen were in need of a pleasant occupation to fill their unaccustomed leisure after an active war career; the Revolution Settlement had been ratified by the Hanoverian Succession; England and Scotland were united and the country set on a course of unprecedented prosperity. No longer could a man be arbitrarily impeached or his property seized for opposition to the state, and the laying out of extensive grounds, as advocated by Addison, with the long-term planting it entailed was a demonstration of faith in the Whig constitution.

Pope was greatly influenced by Addison, who was then the acknowledged monarch of the literary world. Addison had already praised Pope's *Essay on Criticism* as a 'masterpiece of its kind' in his review in 1711 and Pope may well have written the *Guardian* article to impress Addison, who was then in charge of his friend Richard Steele's periodical, with his skill in translating Homer. Addison's call for a gardening reformation provided Pope with the opportunity to insert a long passage in the article translating Homer's description of the gardens of Alcinous; it is certainly more of a poetic exercise than of any particular relevance to garden theory:

> *Close to the Gates a spacious Garden lies,*
> *From Storms defended and inclement Skies:*
> *Four Acres was th'allotted Space of Ground,*
> *Fenc'd with a green Enclosure all around.*
> *Tall thriving Tress confest the fruitful Mold;*
> *The red'ning Apple ripens here to Gold.*[10]

The translation must have impressed Addison, however, as he wrote flatteringly to Pope in 1713 and suggested that he should circulate proposals for a translation of *The Iliad*; which Pope immediately set about doing. The prodigious task of translation, of which Addison said, 'I know of none in this age that is equal to it besides yourself', would take all his energies for the next six years.[11]

Pope had already written a 'Prologue to Mr Addison's Tragedy of Cato', which was performed in April 1713, and he frequented the coffee house where the literary Whigs, Steele, Tickell, Budgell, Garth and Young, sat at Addison's feet in his 'little senate'. Pope stayed frequently in London at the house of his friend Charles Jervas, the portrait painter, from whom he was taking drawing lessons, and by August 1713 he was receiving letters addressed to him 'at Button's Coffee house'. Dryden had gathered the literary wits together at Wills coffee house, but Addison wanted a new meeting place when he was released from duties in the administration after the Whigs fell from power in 1711. He set up his servant Daniel Button in a house in Russell Street as coffee man. Addison had more than conviviality or aristocratic gatherings as at the Kit Cat club in mind; his great crusade was to make the new natural philosophy of the Enlightenment available to a wider public. In *The Spectator* he had said that he was 'ambitious to have it said of me, that I have brought Philosophy out of Closets, Libraries, Schools and Colleges to dwell in Clubs and Assemblies, at Tea-Tables and in Coffee-Houses'.[12]

Addison had spent more than ten years at Oxford and held his fellowship at Magdalen College until 1711. In 1693, as a convinced empiricist, he had given the Encaenia oration on the merits of natural philosophy. To the great natural scientists, of whom Oxford could boast such diligent enquirers as Wren, Boyle, Halley and Hooke, nature was a conceptual whole, the law by which the universe proceeded.[13] Addison was anxious to have the kind of lecture demonstrations that he had profited by in Oxford in his own coffee house and to be able to bring them to wide attention through publication in the periodicals he helped to edit. He first arranged for William Whiston, who had followed Newton as Lucasian professor in Cambridge, to give lectures on Newtonian cosmology at Buttons. Pope attended these in 1713 and 1714. Not having had the chance to be part of an academic community of empiricists, the demonstrations and discussions had a profound effect on him. Whiston's astronomy demonstrations not only developed his interest in telescopes and optics but in the wider aspects of 'the works of Nature'.

Pope wrote deliriously to his friend John Caryll on 14 August 1713:

A plan of a Forest or Rural Garden from Stephen Switzer's *Ichnographia Rustica* of 1718. Switzer disliked the 'diminutive beauties' of Dutch gardening and argued that the whole estate should be part of the garden design. He frequently quoted Addison and Pope in his writings.

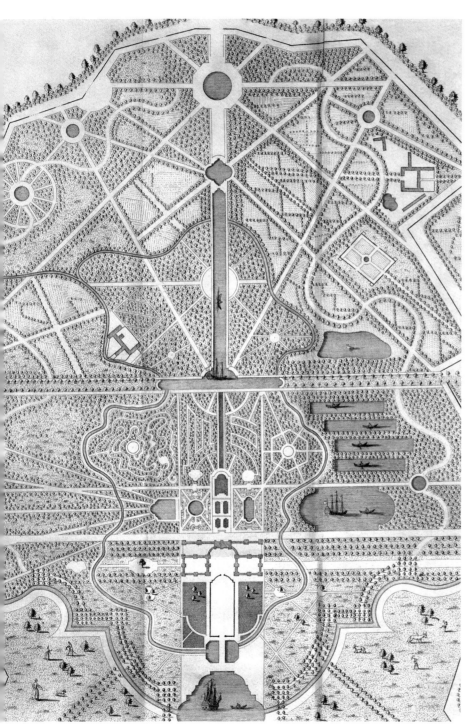

You can't wonder my thoughts are scarce consistent, when I tell you how they are distracted! Every hour of my life my mind is strangely divided. This minute, perhaps, I am above the stars, with a thousand systems round about me, looking forward into the vast abyss of eternity, and losing my whole comprehension in the boundless spaces of the extended Creation, in dialogues with Whiston and the astronomers.[14]

He went on to deplore the 'impiety' of men who could not appreciate a beautiful 'Prospect of Nature'. In this he was following Addison's thinking in *The Spectator* when he first suggested in 1712 that the scientific enquiries and demonstrations on the laws of nature would quicken 'a taste for the Creation' and give a new meaning to the 'Works of Nature'.[15] Addison's suggestion in his 'The Pleasures of the Imagination' articles that 'a beautiful Prospect delights the Soul as much as a Demonstration' had not been lost on Pope.[16]

Addison was a disciple of John Locke, who had recognised that although it was the natural scientists who were advancing knowledge of the universe, the same empirical principles could be applied to the understanding of man's mental faculties. Locke's *Essay Concerning Human Understanding* had been published in 1690 and Addison, whilst still in Magdalen College, Oxford, set himself the task of making a comparable analysis of the imagination. The basis of Addison's aesthetic theory set out in his 'Pleasures of the Imagination' essays, later published in *The Spectator*, was Locke's idea that all knowledge was derived from sense perception and experience; this 'new way of ideas', refuting Plato's innate ideas, was also followed by Pope in his *Essay on Man* in 1733, in which he considered man's place in the universe.

Turning his back on metaphysics and mysticism, Addison, in his relaxed, lucid prose, reassured his *Spectator* readers that there was nothing in the imagination that had not been received by the organ of sight and that by cultivating a 'polite imagination' the faculty of pleasure could be added to ordinary perception and the world seen 'as it were in another Light'.[17] This view was anathema to the later romantic imagination which refused to accept that man was a mere looker-on in an external world. Addison's passive imagination where pleasure could be derived from the contemplation of scenes calculated to arouse polite ideas in the 'Mind of the Beholder' was very influential on the thematic programmes in the early landscape gardens, such as Lord Cobham's Stowe.[18]

Addison encouraged the pursuit of 'innocent pleasures' to stimulate the imagination; these would include architecture, art, statuary, natural scenery and gardening. He went on to say, 'I look upon the Pleasure, which we take in a Garden, as one of the most innocent Delights in Human Life…I cannot but think the very Complacency and Satisfaction which a Man takes in these Works of Nature, to be a laudable, if not a Virtuous Habit of Mind'.[19] It was not long before Pope was in the position to write to a friend that he was himself looking forward to settling down and 'pursuing very innocent pleasures, building, planting and gardening'.[20]

Anthony Ashley Cooper, 3rd Earl of Shaftesbury, went further than Addison by linking aesthetics with the moral sense. He also took the concept of the 'Works of Nature' further from natural science and in *The Moralists* in 1709 he offered a deist kind of nature worship which would not have been out of place a hundred years later:

O GLORIOUS *Nature*! Supremely Fair, and sovereignly Good! All-loving and All-lovely, All-divine!…I shall no longer resist the Passion growing in me for Things of a *natural* kind; where neither *Art*, nor the *Conceit* or *Caprice* of Man has spoil'd their *genuine Order*, by breaking in upon that *primitive State*. Even the rude *Rocks*, the mossy *Caverns*, the irregular unwrought *Grotto's*, and broken *Falls* of Waters, with all the horrid Graces of the *Wilderness* it-self, as representing NATURE more, will be the more engaging, and appear with a Magnificence beyond the formal Mockery of Princely Gardens.[21]

Shaftesbury sought to give the same philosophical background to the arts as had already been allied to scientific thought in Newton's age. In his *Characteristicks* of 1711 he set down his idea that symmetry, proportion and harmony in nature had the same fixed standards in

The woodcut used to illustrate Dryden's translation of the 'Second Pastoral or, Alexis' in *The works of Virgil,* published in 1697 by Jacob Tonson. The illustration was dedicated to Lord Pembroke of Wilton, which was Philip Sidney's 'Arcadia': 'where shepherd boys pipe, as though they would never be old'. Pope, a latterday Alexis, spent long hours 'imaging' Arcadian scenes by 'blest Thames's shores'.

morals. The appreciation of art, architecture and landscape was not then merely a pleasurable sensation but a moral sense. Addison's 'polite imagination' developed into a 'fine taste' which was the new criterion by which every well-bred gentleman would be judged. Shaftesbury died in 1713 and it would be for Lord Burlington to usher in the new concept of taste which would flourish in the stability of the age. Pope was deeply versed in Shaftesbury's moral philosophy and under Lord Burlington's wing would lay out guidelines for the man of taste and good sense, including a system of landscaping which followed nature and consulted the 'Genius of the Place'.

An early nineteenth-century view of Addison's Walk, Magdalen College, Oxford. Addison, a disciple of Locke, wrote most of his essays on 'The Pleasures of the Imagination' when a Fellow, often while enjoying the college's rural walks. Pope, 'bred up at home', was denied a chance 'to hunt for Truth in Maudlin's learned Grove'.

1. Joseph Spence, *Observations, Anecdotes, and Characters of Books and Men*, edited version by James Osborn, 1966, vol.I:24. For Pope's early life see also George Sherburn, *The Early Career of Alexander Pope*, 1934.
2. Addison expresses this view in his 'Essay on the Georgics', published in Dryden's translation of *The Georgics* in 1697.
3. *Correspondence*, 1:168.
4. See Sherburn, *The Early Career of Alexander Pope*, 1934, p.48.
5. *Correspondence*, 1:428.
6. Spence, *Observations*, no.605. See also p.72 below.
7. *Imitations of Horace*, Satire II, Book II, l.135.
8. *The Guardian*, no.173.
9. *The Spectator*, no.253
10. *The Guardian*, no.173. Later published in *Odyssey*, Book III, Twickenham edition, IX, 242-43

11. *Correspondence*, 1:196.
12. *The Spectator*, no.10 (1711).
13. Mavis Batey, *Oxford Gardens*, 1982, p.39.
14. *Correspondence*, 1:288.
15. Mavis Batey, 'The Magdalen Meadows and the Pleasures of the Imagination', *Garden History*, vol.9: no.2 (1981), pp.110-17.
16. *The Spectator*, no.477.
17. Ibid.
18. See George Clarke, 'Grecian Taste and Gothic Virtue: Lord Cobham's Gardening Programme and its Iconography', *Apollo*, 97 (June 1973), pp.566-71.
19. *The Spectator*, no.477.
20. *Correspondence*, 2:3.
21. Shaftesbury, *The Moralists*, 1709, in *Characteristics*, ed. J.M.Robertson, 1964, III, ii, p.125.

'UNDER THE WING OF MY LORD BURLINGTON'

Chiswick: *View of the Temple by the Water* by Jacques Rigaud.
The hunchbacked figure enjoying the music in the foreground is
clearly intended to be Pope, who frequently visited Chiswick
even after he had moved five miles up the river to Twickenham.
'I assure you Chiswick has been to me the finest thing this
glorious sun has shined on', Pope would write in 1732.

Y ou show us, Rome was glorious, not profuse,
And pompous buildings once were things of Use,
Yet shall (my Lord) your just, your noble rules
Fill half the land with Imitating Fools;
Who random drawings from your sheets shall take,
And of one beauty many blunders make;
Load some vain Church with old Theatric state,
Turn Arcs of triumph to a Garden-gate;
Reverse your Ornaments, and hang them all
On some patch'd dog-hole ek'd with ends of wall,
Then clap four slices of Pilaster on't,
That, lac'd with bits of rustic, makes a Front,
Or call the winds thro' long Arcades to roar,
Proud to catch cold at a Venetian door;
Conscious they act a true Palladian part,
And if they starve, they starve by rules of art.
Oft have you hinted to your brother Peer,
A certain truth, which many buy too dear:
Something there is more needful than Expence,
And something previous ev'n to Taste - 'tis Sense:
Good Sense, which only is the gift of Heav'n,
And tho' no science, fairly worth the sev'n:
A Light, which in yourself you must perceive;
Jones and Le Nôtre have it not to give.

Alexander Pope: *Epistle IV. To Richard Boyle, Earl of Burlington:*
Of the Use of Riches, 1731, lines 23-46.

RICHARD BOYLE, THIRD EARL OF BURLINGTON, was the greatest patron and arbiter of taste of the Georgian era. He was only ten years old when, in 1704, he succeeded to the title and valuable family estates in London, Chiswick, Yorkshire and Ireland. When Queen Anne died in 1714, he was given office with the second generation of Whigs, who came to power in the Hanoverian succession, but he had little interest in affairs of state. The young Burlington was bent on taking up Shaftesbury's challenge to elevate the status of the arts to that of science and to institute an academy of arts to rival the Royal Society. 'Belov'd of every Muse', as John Gay said of him in 1715, the wealthy young aristocrat was well placed to carry through the Shaftesbury-based Whig aspirations of a 'national taste'. In Alexander Pope, the rising literary star, Burlington found the perfect publicist for his mission of relating morals and good taste; and, more importantly, one who was also acquiring an ability to ridicule false taste.

It was Pope's *Essay on Criticism*, published in 1711, which would already have attracted the young Burlington. Addison had said that Pope's observations were given with 'elegance and Perspicuity', and Dr Johnson thought that although the essay was written by such a young man, 'if he had written nothing else would have placed him among the first critics and the first poets'.[1] Pope's essay was an exposition on the rules of taste and the authority to be attributed to the ancients. Burlington would perhaps have seen a role for himself in Pope's argument that 'a true Taste is as rare to be found, as a true Genius' and that there were those 'born to Judge, as well as those to Write'. A critic need not be exclusively a writer like Horace, Boileau or young Pope, it seemed; there would also be an important role for a connoisseur, a word that was invented for the new critic of the fine arts in the Burlington age.

Burlington brought back presents for Pope from his first Grand Tour in 1715 and by April of the next year had settled him and his parents, under his wing, in Mawsons New Buildings near his house at Chiswick, where the poet was able to enjoy a new lifestyle. Living only five miles from London also gave him easier access to his publishers and bookseller. Pope had made a preliminary visit to Chiswick and wrote excitedly to Martha Blount in March, 'I am to pass three or four days in high luxury, with some company at my Lord Burlington's; We are to walk, ride, ramble, dine, drink and lye together. His gardens are delightfull, his musick ravishing'.[2] The music at Chiswick House would have been provided by Handel whom the earl had installed at Burlington House, together with the sculptor Guelfi, on his return from his Grand Tour.

Pope was well settled at Chiswick by 9 July when he wrote of his patron to his friend Charles Jervas:

My Lord Burlington desires you may be put in mind of him. His gardens flourish, his structures rise, his pictures arrive, and (what is far nobler and more valuable than all) his own good qualities daily extend themselves to all about him: Whereof, I the meanest (next to some Italian chymists, fidlers, bricklayers, and opera-makers) am a living instance.[3]

According to John Gay the diminutive Pope also enjoyed his Lordship's fruit 'within his reach':

While you, my Lord, bid stately Piles ascend,
Or in your Chiswick Bow'rs enjoy your Friend;
Where Pope unloads the Bough within his reach
Of purple Grape, blue Plumb, or blushing Peach.[4]

Burlington House, with its 'laborious Lobster-nights',[5] was also at Pope's disposal. The earl's friends were encouraged to come and go at will to his private academy of arts even in his absence. Pope would soon have been caught up with Lord Burlington's new passion for Palladian architecture. In 1715 Leoni's translation of Palladio's *Quattro Libri* and the first volume of Colen Campbell's *Vitruvius Britannicus*, containing

Earl of Burlington

Left. Jonathan Richardson's portrait of Richard Boyle, 3rd Earl of Burlington, standing proudly in front of the Bagnio of 1717, which was 'the first essay of his Lordship's happy invention'. Pope was living in Chiswick at the time; his knowledge of the classics was of great value to the Burlington set in their search for 'ancient rules' to formulate taste.

Below. William Kent as painted by Benedetto Luti while in Rome in 1718. Kent was to return with Burlington the following year to spend the rest of his life as his colleague and friend.

illustrations of British buildings based on Roman models, appeared. Burlington immediately espoused the Palladian cause and soon became its acknowledged leader. His ambition was to revive the Vitruvian principles of Augustan Rome and to restore Palladian architecture to the position it had held before the Civil War in the time of Inigo Jones. In the words of Pope, Burlington's new mission was to:

Erect new wonders, and the old repair;
Jones and Palladio to themselves restore,
And be whate'er Vitruvius was before.[6]

Colen Campbell, who had become the earl's mentor, was instructed to take over from Gibbs at Burlington House and remodel it as a new Palladian palazzo. The earl set off on a second Italian tour in 1719, this time with the specific intention of studying in depth Palladio's villas near Vicenza and to obtain whatever drawings and papers of the master were still available. He returned home, not only with manuscripts, but with a new protégé who would be a lifelong friend and partner – William Kent. He was immediately installed at Burlington House, where he remained until his death in 1748, when he was buried in the family vault at Chiswick. Burlington had the highest regard for Kent's abilities and lost no time in bringing Kent 'the painter', as he was then referred to, and Pope together to their great mutual advantage.

Pope's knowledge of classical writings was of great value to the Burlington set seeking the 'right models' of antiquity to formulate taste. His advice in his *Essay on Criticism* had been: 'Learn hence for Ancient Rules a just Esteem'.[7] In terms of architecture there were books of Vitruvius and Palladio to follow and the earl brought back ideas from Palladio's own Villa Rotonda for the new villa he was planning to build adjacent to Chiswick House. When Burlington came to consider reviving classical gardening, however, there was no such authority for authentic gardens of the ancients, although he would have seen Italian Renaissance gardens when on his tour.[8] In his *Vitruvius Britannicus*, in 1715, Campbell had condemned the 'capricious ornaments' of baroque

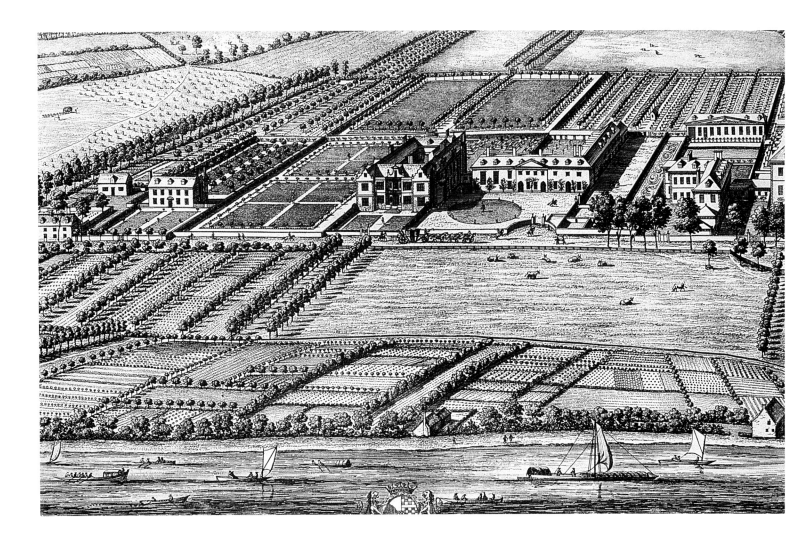

architecture and praised 'antique simplicity' at the same time as Pope was advocating 'amiable simplicity' as 'the Taste of the Ancients in their gardens' in his article in *The Guardian*.

Pope was relying on general classical precepts rather than giving any real information about ancient garden design and there was a strong moral note about his 'simplicity', which he had defined as 'the mean between ostentation and rusticity'. The aim was Horace's theme of *simplex munditiis*, taken from the imagery of the modest fair youth who neither wore false ornaments nor left his hair unkempt, but simply braided his tresses elegantly; in gardening terms Pope would see this as:

In all, let Nature never be forgot.
But treat the Goddess like a modest fair
Nor over-dress, nor leave her wholly bare.[9]

Stephen Switzer, who used *simplex munditiis* as one of his gardening precepts, had been able to adapt not only Horace's dicta for his own purposes but also early remarks of Pope. He quoted Pope's edict 'First follow Nature' from his *Essay on Criticism*, published in 1711, as part of his garden theory, although Pope's Nature then had more to do with Newton than any natural garden design; nor had the poet intended his general statement on naturalness in conduct, based on a 'just esteem for

Old Chiswick House in a bird's-eye view of *c.*1698-99 by Johannes Kip after Knyff showing the squared gardens Burlington inherited. These would be transformed by irregular gardening, Pope's 'Order in Variety', which he began to experiment with at Twickenham in 1719.

ancient rules', to be applied to gardening. Undaunted Switzer merely substituted Pope's 'wit' for 'gardens' to arrive at a plausible integrated landscape design for those noblemen and gentlemen laying out extensive grounds at the end of the Marlborough Wars:

> *Survey the Whole....*
> *In Gardens* [Pope's wit], *as Nature, what affects our hearts*
> *Is not th' exactness of peculiar parts;*
> *'Tis not a lip, or eye, we beauty call,*
> *But the joint force and full result of all.*
> *No single parts unequally surprise,*
> *All comes united to th' admiring eyes.*[10]

Classical descriptions of gardens were the only real guide to what 'simplicity' might be, however, and they were far from clear. Pope had poured scorn on topiary, made popular by Dutch gardening under William III, in his pleas in the *Guardian* article for the 'amiable Simplicity of unadorned Nature', which he claimed was the 'Taste of the Ancients':

How contrary to this Simplicity is the modern Practice of Gardening; we seem to make it our Study to recede from Nature, not only in the various Tonsure of Greens into the most regular and formal Shapes, but even in monstrous Attempts beyond the reach of Art itself; We run into Sculpture, and are better pleas'd to have our Trees in the most awkward Figures of Men and Animals, than in the most regular of their own.[11]

The Villa Rotonda, near Vicenza, designed by Palladio in 1550. Burlington's second Grand Tour in 1719 was undertaken specifically to study Palladian villas in the Veneto.

Above. Chiswick House: The Pond and the Temple, circa 1729-31.

Right. Detail of the landscape setting behind the Bagnio at Chiswick
from Rysbrack's *A View of Chiswick Gardens towards the rear of the Bagnio.*

However, gardeners were called *topiarii* in Rome because of their skill in clipping trees and hedges into curious forms; these were called 'tonsile evergreens' by Pliny the Younger, who described with pleasure the various forms of animals artfully represented alongside the master's name in box.

The gardens and orchard which Pope had enjoyed as Burlington's neighbour belonged to the old Jacobean Chiswick House. The earl's chief interest at the time was displaying his garden buildings in a theatrical way as the focal point of his garden layout. The bagnio, 'the first essay of his Lordship's happy invention', according to Campbell, was designed before he went on his second Grand Tour in 1719. He was obviously delighted with his handiwork, which figures in the background to his portrait. Chiswick Villa, which according to Defoe surpassed 'everything of its kind in England, if not Europe',[12] was begun in 1726 after a fire in the old house; it had at its entrance flanking statues of Burlington's mentors Palladio and Inigo Jones. 'Who builds like Boyle', cried Pope admiringly in his *Epistle to the Earl of Burlington*. He could not resist teasing him, however, about the

Above. William Kent's drawing of the entrance front at Chiswick shows the statue of Burlington's mentor Andrea Palladio (Inigo Jones stands on the other side of the entrance).

Previous page. Inigo Jones's gate was brought from Beaufort House, Chelsea, to Chiswick in 1738.

Above. Chiswick House garden front. Originally old Chiswick House and the new villa were unconnected; it was not until 1733 that the link building was added.

Right. The orange tree garden at Chiswick. Burlington's Ionic Temple by the circular pond was completed in 1728.

unsuitability of Palladian through draughts in the English climate:

Or call the winds thro' long Arcades to roar,
Proud to catch cold at a Venetian door;
Conscious they act a true Palladian part,
And if they starve, they starve by rules of art.[13]

There was much to give pleasure to the 'Mind of the Beholder' wishing to cultivate Addison's 'polite imagination'. The garden celebrated classical taste through statues of Palladio and Jones. The portico of the pavilion by the geometrical basin was a miniature of that at Inigo Jones's St Paul's, Covent Garden. Inigo Jones's own gateway was later brought from Beaufort House. Lord Burlington also designed the Ionic Temple, with columns based on one in Rome, by the round pond with the central obelisk. In 1724 John Macky said that the whole contrivance of the gardens 'is the effect of his Lordship's own genius, and singular fine taste'.[14] In the 1730s, however, when William Kent, influenced by Pope, embarked on 'a new taste in gardening', Lord Burlington's Chiswick gardens would be modified accordingly, although still paying respect to the 'taste of the ancients'.

Pope's own gardening ideas would not take root until he had his own garden in which to try them out, but while still at Chiswick he went on a round of country house visiting, where gardens were in the making. In August 1717 he wrote to his friend, John Caryll of Ladyholt, Sussex:

After some attendance on my Lord Burlington, I have been at the Duke of Shrewsbury's, Duke of Argyll's, Lady Rochester's, Lord Perceval's, Mr Stoner's, Lord Winchelsea's, Sir Godfrey Kneller (who has made me a fine present of a picture) and Duchess Hamilton's. All these indispensable claims to me, under penalty of the imputation of direct rudeness, living within two hours sail of Chiswick. Then am I obliged to pass some days between my Lord Bathurst's and three or four more on the Windsor side. Thence to Mr Dancaster, and my relations at Bagshot Heath. I am also promised three months ago to the Bishop of Rochester's for three days on the other side of the water.[15]

Pope's pocket Homer would have to accompany him wherever he went as he was still deeply engrossed in translating *The Iliad*. He had undertaken to the publisher to produce six volumes, one a year, the first of which appeared in 1715. The summer of 1718 was spent between Lord Bathurst's Cirencester Park and Stanton Harcourt in Oxfordshire. A tower in the Harcourts' partly ruined manor house was rehabilitated for Pope as a study and it was here, in what is now called Pope's Tower, that he recorded on a pane of window glass that the fifth volume of *The Iliad* was finished in that room. The glass was later

Godfrey Kneller's portrait of Pope painted in 1719 with the *The Iliad* on his knee. Pope's pocket edition of Homer's *Iliad* travelled everywhere with him. Horace Walpole later acquired it to put on display in his Strawberry Hill library.

removed and taken to the Harcourts' new house at Nuneham Courtenay. However laborious the translations were, Pope was amassing quite an income from them, as he was paid 200 guineas a volume with 750 free copies which he could distribute as he liked.

Pope's father died in October 1717 and with the proceeds from *The Iliad* Pope decided to set up house with his widowed mother to enjoy his own lifestyle and circle of friends in a new establishment. Burlington offered a plot behind his house in Piccadilly, which would have given easier access to London life. Pope gave this some thought and went so far as to have plans made, but in the aftermath of the 1715 Rebellion there was considerable anti-Jacobite tension with the fear that the relaxed rule preventing Roman Catholics from living within ten miles of London might be enforced. Pope gave his reason for

seeking a rural retreat in his *Imitations of Horace*, claiming that he shunned 'crowds and courts' and preferred, like the Augustan poet, to retire to 'grottos and to groves'. Soon he was writing to tell his friends that 'The Gods and fate have fix'd me on the borders of the Thames, in the Districts of Richmond and Twickenham'.[16]

In February 1719 Pope wrote to Lord Burlington, who was then at Chatsworth, 'I'm sure you shall always have me for your Neighbor, wherever I live'.[17] Pope no longer needed patronage, but the years 'under the Wing of my Lord Burlington' had been very important to him and the association would continue for the rest of his life. The advantages of the friendship were mutual and in 1732 Lord Burlington ended a letter to Pope, 'I never can leave off without reassuring you that no mortal can be with more affection than I am my dear friend'.[18]

Pope in the study made for him in the tower of the ruined manor of Stanton Harcourt. He recorded on a window pane that the fifth volume of *The Iliad* was completed there.

1. *The Spectator*, no. 253; Samuel Johnson, *The Lives of the English Poets*, ed. G.B.Hill, 1905, III, p.228.
2. *Correspondence*, 1:338.
3. *Correspondence*, 1:347.
4. John Gay, *Poetry and Prose*, ed. Vinton A. Dearing, 1972, vol.2, p.203.
5. TE VI p.130, l.45.
6. *Epistle IV. To Richard Boyle, Earl of Burlington*, 1731, ll.192-94.
7. *Essay on Criticism*, l.139.
8. See John Dixon Hunt, *Garden and Grove*, 1986, for an account of Italian Renaissance gardens seen on the Grand Tour.
9. Horace, *Odes*, Book I, V, for *simplex munditiis*. Pope's *Epistle to the Earl of Burlinton*, ll.50-52.
10. Stephen Switzer, *Ichnographia Rustica*, 1718, preface xxi.
11. *The Spectator*, no.173.
12. Daniel Defoe, *A tour through the whole island of Great Britain*, 1742, vol.3, p.287.
13. *Epistle to the Earl of Burlington*, ll.35-38.
14. John Macky, *A journey through England...*, 1724, vol.1, p.87.
15. *Correspondence*, 1:417
16. *Correspondence*, 2:24.
17. *Correspondence*, 2:11.
18. *Correspondence*, 3:323.

'HAPPY THE MAN'

Peter Tillemans, *The Thames at Twickenham, circa* 1730, with
Pope's villa the dominant building. 'The Gods and fate have fix'd
me on the borders of the Thames, in the Districts of Richmond
and Twickenham', Pope wrote with satisfaction in 1719.
Twickenham soon became known as the 'classic village'.

Content with little, I can piddle here
On Broccoli and mutton, round the year;
But ancient friends, (tho' poor, or out of play)
That touch my bell, I cannot turn away.
'Tis true, no Turbots dignify my boards,
But gudgeons, flounders, what my Thames affords;
To Hounslow-heath I point, and Bansted-down,
Thence comes your mutton, and these chicks my own:
From yon old walnut-tree a show'r shall fall;
And grapes, long lingring on my only wall,
And figs, from standard and Espalier join;
The dev'l is in you if you cannot dine.
Then chearful healths (your Mistress shall have place)
And, what's more rare, a Poet shall say Grace.

Alexander Pope: *The Second Satire of the Second Book of Horace Imitated, to Mr. Bethel,* 1734, lines 137-50.

His House, embosom'd in the Grove,
Sacred to social life and social Love,
Shall glitter o'er the pendent green,
Where Thames reflects the visionary Scene.

Alexander Pope: *Imitations of Horace,* Book IV, Ode 1, lines 21-24

ALEXANDER POPE settled in Twickenham in 1719 and set up court there for twenty five years in the image of his own cultural beliefs, based on classical precepts, poetic sensibility and a moral sense. He had come to terms with the restrictions that his deformity and frailty imposed upon his activities and his life was necessarily fulfilled by his writing, translations and imitations of the classics, moralising, friendships, gardening and grotto-making; everything he did was polished and refined to perfection. Pope's personality and his lifestyle acted as a magnet for the major literary figures of the day. Voltaire, Bolingbroke, Swift and Gay stayed in his riverside villa and he was visited by Frederick, Prince of Wales. His praise was widely courted and the ridicule of the author of *The Dunciad* came to be dreaded.

Pope's lines on Twickenham, which he wrote before 1709 in a juvenile poem parodying Spenser, were prophetic. When recalling the Thames he knew as a boy in the city, he writes of the more salubrious upstream Twickenham and its riverside gardens. In ten years time he would be enriching its 'fairer scenes' by making a notable contribution with his own garden and grotto.

> *Such place hath Deptford, navy-building Town,*
> *Woolwich and Wapping, smelling strong of Pitch;*
> *Such Lambeth, envy of each band and gown,*
> *And Twick'nam such, which fairer scenes enrich,*
> *Grots, statues, urns, and Johnston's Dog and Bitch.*[1]

The Twickenham and Richmond area had long been fashionable with courtiers and city men, not only to take advantage of the delights of the royal park and a riverside setting, but because the Thames provided easy transport to London and Hampton Court. In the eighteenth century it developed a character all of its own as a rural retreat that attracted poets, painters, actors, architects, gardeners and musicians.[2] Lady Mary Wortley Montagu, who with her husband, after their return from Turkey, stayed with Pope in 1719 while house-hunting, found she could pass her time in Twickenham 'in great indolence and sweetness' with more freedom for cultural pursuits and more reasonable hours than prevailed in London with its nightly assemblies, balls and card-playing. The inhabitants of this little 'Kingdom...on the banks of the Thames' of which Pope was soon to become monarch had the freedom of fellow residents' gardens, harpsichords and libraries. The closeness of Pope and Lady Mary was talked about after the Wortleys had found a neighbouring property, but it was an indication of their 'gallant' relationship that she had borrowed Philip Sidney's *Arcadia* from Pope.[3]

The part of Twickenham called Cross Deep where Pope took a lease of a small house from Thomas Vernon also had a small artisan community including a tannery next door.[4] He lost no time, however, in converting the modest property into a villa. Although Lord Burlington had not as yet begun his Chiswick villa, Pope had had the benefit of seeing his books illustrating Palladian architecture and discussing with him ideas on the appropriate aesthetic setting for a cultivated man in villa retirement. James Gibbs helped with draughts and elevations for the house, but Pope was much involved with the masons himself. He told a friend in July 1720 that he was on a diet of 'Water-gruel and Palladio'[5] and Burlington's advice was constantly sought. The earl also helped by supplying building materials and Pope acknowledged gratefully that he had commanded that 'there should be nothing Durable in my building, which I was not to owe to Chiswick'.[6]

The drudgery of the *Iliad* translations was over by the summer of 1720 when Pope was building his villa and Gay wrote his 'Mr Pope's Welcome from Greece'. Five years later he would publish a translation of the *Odyssey* but this was not so exacting as it was more of a collaborative venture. Although Pope still sealed his letters with a head of Homer, mindful that it was thanks to him he could 'live and thrive / indebted to no prince or peer

alive',[7] it was Horace who would henceforth be imitated. 'I cough like Horace',[8] he boasted and doubtless preoccupation with Horace's Sabine farm was much more suited to villa retirement than the wanderings of Greek heroes.

Pope felt at one with Horace and Cicero, who associated their country retreats with contemplative study and poetic composition, and he frequently referred to his Twickenham retreat as 'my Tusculum' after Cicero's villa outside Rome. Twickenham, linked with Pope's ideas, soon became known as the 'classic village'. Pope's own version of Horace's 'Beatus ille' image was:

Happy the man who to the shades retires,
But doubly happy, if the Muse inspires!
Blest whom the sweets of home-felt quiet please;
But far more blest, who study joins with ease.[9]

'Happy the man' it was indeed for Pope, who could say with Horace, 'This used to be among my prayers – a portion of land not so very large, but which should contain a garden, and near the homestead ever-flowing water and a piece of forest to complete it'.[10] Pope also rejoiced in achieving the Horatian ambition:

I've often wish'd that I had clear
For life, six hundred pounds a year,
A handsome House to lodge a Friend,
A River at my garden's end,
A Terras-walk, and half a Rood
Of Land set out to plant a Wood.[11]

A 'River at my garden's end', particularly a navigable one, was a true requisite of a Palladian villa and the many views of Pope's villa show his waterborne guests arriving at his riverside lawn. This was only small and very public, however, and Pope took five acres of agricultural land across the Hampton Court road in stages to make a new garden. 'Gardening is near-akin to Philosophy', he said,[12] and it had been a cherished wish to create a garden based on the ideas he had formed at Binfield, with Lord Burlington at Chiswick, and when visiting his friends' country estates.

Pope's villa in an engraving by N.Parr after a drawing of about 1735 by Pieter Rysbrack. Pope called his villa 'my Tusculum' and set up court for twenty-five years in the image of his own cultural beliefs, based on classical precepts, poetic sensibility and a moral sense.

Alfred's Hall, Cirencester, was designed by Pope and Lord Bathurst in 1721. It was the first purpose-built gothic ruin and lay deep in the woods.

In October 1720 Pope obtained permission to excavate a tunnel under the road for access to the garden and to connect it with the underground grotto, which was to be an essential part of the overall design. Dr Johnson, who was no grotto admirer, observed that he had 'extracted an ornament from an inconvenience, and vanity provided a grotto where necessity enforced a passage'.[13] Pope's friend Swift was more complimentary and in 1725 told the latter-day Horace that he had achieved much in his building and planting and especially in the 'Subterranean Passage to your Garden whereby you turned a blunder into a beauty which is a piece of Ars Poetica'.[14] At its entrance Pope placed an inscription from Horace, who also had a grotto on his Sabine farm, 'Secretum iter et fallentis semita vitae' (A hid Recess,

where Life's revolving Day/In sweet Delusion gently steals away).[15]

Pope was anxious to share these sweet delusions with his friends in his 'Twitnam bowers' dedicated to 'social life and social love'. Swift said that it was Pope who 'taught me to dream…now I can every night distinctly see Twitenham and the Grotto'.[16] Another early visitor to Twickenham was Robert Digby of Sherborne in Dorset, who in the summer of 1723, on his return home, thanks his host 'heartily for the new agreeable idea of life you there gave me and it will remain long with me, for it is very strongly impressed on my imagination. I repeat the memory of it often, and shall value that faculty of the mind now more than ever'.[17] These were the pleasures of the imagination that Addison had recommended to the

readers of *The Spectator*. He had by then left the scene but Pope was able to offer a whole new lifestyle which would add the faculty of pleasure to perception through poetic imagination.

Robert Digby and Pope had for many years been intimate friends of Lord Bathurst and had frequently walked together in Cirencester's 'enchanted Forest', where Pope, who had his own 'sylvan seat' there, said, 'I look upon myself as the Magician appropriated to the place, without whom no mortal can penetrate the Recesses of these sacred Shades'.[18] Bathurst's forest glades had compensated him for the loss of Windsor Forest when he moved to Chiswick. In 1721 Pope and Bathurst designed Alfred's Hall, the first purpose-built ruin, in the depth of the woods and were delighted a few years later when it was taken by an antiquarian to be a genuine relic of Alfred's time. Pope had opened up ideas of romantic gothic scenes in his *Eloisa to Abelard* of 1717 by placing the tragic heroine in a Miltonic landscape with awful cells and twilight groves. Hermitages, towers, ruins and caverns soon appeared even in the parks of hunting squires.

Robert Digby had learned from Pope to cherish a 'solemn scene' but he needed no fictitious commemorative ruins to recall the heroic past. At Sherborne he possessed the original old castle of the Raleighs, left to ruin when Sir Walter built a new house across the river Yeo, in which the Digby family lived.[19] Even before he visited Sherborne himself Pope had encouraged Digby to revere his ancestors and their ruins, particularly Raleigh who had been Edmund Spenser's patron. On his return to Sherborne in 1723 Digby wrote to Pope, 'I have as you guess, many philosophical reveries in the shades of Sir Walter Raleigh, of which you are a great part. You generally enter there with me, and like a good Genius applaud and strengthen all my sentiments that have honour in them'.[20] Pope's poetic sensibility had given him a sense of place through the imaginative appreciation of Raleigh's Sherborne landscape.

More sophisticated pleasures of the imagination were taking place near Pope at Richmond, where the royal court indulged in Arcadian fêtes galantes. The Prince and Princess of Wales, having quarrelled with George I, had taken up residence at Richmond Lodge as a royal retreat the same year as Pope settled in Twickenham. Princess Caroline was anxious to improve her riverside gardens and in 1719 called a conference of 'gardening lords' to which Pope was invited. Although he had not, as yet, begun his own garden, the court would have known from Lord Burlington of Pope's interest in gardening. Although he would have been invited to the fêtes galantes his frail constitution would not have permitted him to indulge in such robust outdoor activities.

The idea of the fête galante had come to England through the paintings of Watteau, who was himself in London in 1719, and engravings of his enchanting park scenes were soon available. Caroline's court, which was also enamoured of the pastorals of Pope and Gay, was invited to relive Watteau's golden world of picnics, minuets, coquetries and masquerades in the Richmond gardens. It seems the fêtes galantes were not all as sunlit as Watteau would have us suppose; Lady Mary Wortley Montagu described to her sister in 1723 the miseries of Thames Arcadia at Richmond in inclement weather:

You may imagine poor Galantry droops except in the Elysian shades of Richmond. There is no such thing as Love or Pleasure. Tis said there is a fine lady retir'd from having taken too much on it. For my part they are not all cook'd to my taste and I have very little share in the diversion there.[21]

The fine lady in question might have been the Duchess of Queensberry from nearby Douglas House, who boasted that she could milk a cow and had her portrait painted by Jervas in the guise of a milkmaid. Horace Walpole delighted in the absurdity of people of fashion and rank playing 'a kind of impossible pastoral, a rural life led by those opposites of rural simplicity'. John Gay, on the suggestion of Swift and under the patronage of the pastoral Duchess of Queensberry, would extend the idea that appreciating the simple feelings of the lower orders would be beneficial even for courtiers into his Newgate pastoral, *The Beggar's Opera*, in 1728.

Chatelain's view, based on Watteau's *Pilgrimage to Cythera*, shows the Richmond court pretending to be natural in a fête galante. The pilgrimage is to Syon House on the other bank.

A striking example of the court imitating the simple life is the view of the royal gardens by the Thames engraved by Chatelain with unmistakable figures from Watteau's *Pilgrimage to Cythera*, which was also called '*une feste galante*'. Lord Shaftesbury had already hinted at such behaviour in *The Moralists* as early as 1709, when he praised 'Things of a *natural* kind' rather than parading in 'the formal Mockery of Princely Gardens' and asked, 'But tell me, I intreat you, how comes it that, excepting a few Philosophers of your sort, the only People who are enam-

our'd in this way and seek the Woods, the Rivers, or Sea-Shores, are yon poor vulgar lovers?'[22]

Pope could now exchange the imaginary nymphs and shepherds of Windsor Forest for real pastoral ladies who frequented 'happy bowers' along the Thames. Chief amongst these, once he had broken with his infatuation for Lady Mary Wortley Montagu, was the Prince of Wales's official mistress, Henrietta Howard, later the Countess of Suffolk, who was the Chloe of his eclogues. Although Pope did not see himself, like Lord

Peterborough, as her 'gallant' he did pay mock court to her, at noon, her appointed hour of reception at her Woman of the Bedchamber lodgings at Richmond. It was around 1720, according to Lord Harvey, when the future George II began to spend 'every evening of his life, three or four hours' with Mrs Howard. By all accounts this 'reasonable woman', as Pope called her, knew how to deal with her admirers, as the poet, mocking her deafness, writes in 'On a certain Lady at Court':

> *I know the thing that's most uncommon;*
> *(Envy be silent, and attend!)*
> *I know a Reasonable Woman,*
> *Handsome and witty, yet a Friend.*
>
> *Not warp'd by Passion, aw'd by Rumour.*
> *Not grave thro' Pride, or gay thro' Folly,*
> *An equal mixture of good Humour,*
> *And sensible soft Melancholy.*
>
> *'Has she no faults then (Envy says) Sir?'*
> *Yes, she has one, I must aver;*
> *When all the World conspires to praise her,*
> *The Woman's deaf, and does not hear.*

In 1724 the Prince of Wales would advance the money for Henrietta Howard to build a villa for herself at Twickenham, where she could live away from her estranged husband and have some independence. Pope revelled in the idea of assisting her (see below, Chapter 6). The poet was also involved with helping his great friend Henry St John Bolingbroke to settle near him at Dawley. After the accession of George I and the resurgence of the Whigs, Bolingbroke had fled to France and declared his allegiance to the Pretender, James Stuart. He returned to England in 1725, with a limited pardon, having previously stayed with Pope discreetly while looking for a suitable new estate. With the help of Lord Bathurst, whose Middlesex estate Riskins (or Richings) was near Colnbrook, Bolingbroke acquired nearby Dawley Manor, situated about four miles from Twickenham.[23]

Bolingbroke renamed the manor Dawley Farm and announced his intention of becoming a philosopher-

Henrietta Howard
(1688-1767). She later
became Countess of
Suffolk and was the
official mistress of the
Prince of Wales (later
George II) and lady-in-
waiting to the Princess.
Pope paid mock court
to this 'reasonable
woman' at Richmond
and she became the
Chloe of his eclogues.

farmer, devoted to classical husbandry and public virtue. Pope wrote to Swift, somewhat wryly sitting by a haystack , 'Now his Lordship is run after his Cart, I have a moment left to myself to tell you that I overheard him yesterday agree with a Painter for 200 l. to paint his country hall with Trophies of Rakes, spades, prongs etc. and other ornaments merely to countenance his calling this place a Farm'.[24] As Pope was aware, Dawley's ostentatious good husbandry was largely a Tory political gesture against Whig corruption and misuse of wealth, which Pope would later take up in the argument on 'the vanity of expense' of 'Timon's villa' in his *Epistle to the Earl of Burlington*.

Although Pope had no land on which to practise such classical husbandry he did keep bees and bantams,

cultivate a good vegetable garden and grow pineapples.[25] Addressing himself to his countryman friend, Bethel, whom he compared to Horace's philosopher-farmer Ofellus, Pope spoke of his own modest self-sufficiency and homespun hospitality:

Content with little, I can piddle here
On Broccoli and mutton, round the year.[26]

Visits to the city were not excluded from Pope's 'Beatus ille' rural life, but the poet always returned with thankfulness to his Twickenham retreat, and particularly to his grotto, which had become the focus of his spiritual life.

Thoughts, which at Hyde-Park-Corner I forgot,
Meet and rejoin me, in the pensive Grot.[27]

John Gay's summer-
house. The Duchess of
Queensberry was the
patron of Pope's friend
and fellow poet John
Gay, for whom she built
a summerhouse by the
Thames at her
Petersham house. There
he wrote *The Beggar's
Opera* and adapted
Virgil's pastoral
eclogues into satiric
town eclogues.

1.   *Imitations of English Poets*, II. 'Spenser, The Alley'. Written before 1709, but these lines were possibly added before publication in 1727. See p.73 for Johnston's statues.
2.   See Mavis Batey *et al.*, *Arcadian Thames*, 1994, pp.76-77.
3.   R.Halsband, *The Life of Lady Mary Wortley Montagu*, 1956, pp. 106 and 114.
4.   A.Beckles Willson, *Mr Pope & Others*, 1996.
5.   *Correspondence*, 2:50.
6.   *Correspondence*, 3:341.
7.   *Imitations of Horace*, Epistle II, Book II, ll.68-69.
8.   *Epistle to Dr. Arbuthnot*, l.116.
9.   Horace, *Epodes*, II.
10. Horace, *Satires II*, VI, ll.1-3
11. *Imitations of Horace*, Book II, Satire VI, ll.1-6.
12. *Correspondence*, 4:6.
13. *The Works of Samuel Johnson*, ed. R.Lynam, 1825, vol.IV, p.199.
14. *Correspondence*, 2:325-26.
15. Horace, *Epistles*, I, XVIII, 103.
16. *Correspondence*, 3:393.
17. *Correspondence*, 2:191.
18. *Correspondence*, 2: 115.
19. For Sherborne see Peter Martin, 'Intimations of the New Gardening: Alexander Pope's reaction to the 'uncommon' landscape at Sherborne', *Garden History*, vol.4, no.1 (1976), pp.57-87.
20. *Correspondence*, 2:192.
21. R. Halsband, *The Complete Letters of Lady Mary Wortley Montagu*, vol.II, p.30.
22. For Richmond fêtes galantes see *Arcadian Thames*, pp.102-5.
23. For Dawley see David Jacques, 'The Art and Sense of the Scriblerus Club', *Garden History*, vol.4, no.1 (1976) pp.30-53.
24. *Correspondence*, 2:503.
25. For an excellent appraisal of Pope's classical lifestyle and retirement see Maynard Mack, *The Garden and the City*, 1969.
26. *Imitations of Horace*, Satire II, Book II, ll.137-38.
27. *Imitations of Horace*, Epistle II, Book II, ll.208-9.

'THE PENSIVE GROT'

The grotto of the nymph Egeria was a popular stop on the
Grand Tour. Spence brought back fragments of marble
from it for Pope's grotto.

*T*hou who shalt stop, where Thames' translucent Wave

Shines a broad Mirrour thro' the shadowy Cave;

Where ling'ring Drops from Mineral Roofs distill,

And pointed Crystals break the sparkling Rill,

Unpolish'd Gemms no Ray on Pride bestow,

And latent Metals innocently glow:

Approach. Great NATURE studiously behold!

And eye the Mine without a Wish for Gold.

Approach: But aweful! Lo th'AEgerian *Grott*,

Where, nobly-pensive, ST. JOHN sate and thought;

Where British *Sighs from dying* WYNDHAM stole,

And the bright Flame was shot thro' MARCHMONT's Soul

Let such, such only, tread this sacred Floor,

Who dare to love their Country, and be poor.

Alexander Pope: 'Verses on a Grotto by the River Thames at Twickenham,
composed of Marbles, Spars and Minerals', 1740 (published 1741).

POPE'S GROTTO, AND HIS GARDEN, WERE A
source of inspiration and contentment for him. Martha
Blount, who was to inherit urns from his garden and
movable effects from the grotto, said that the latter was
his only extravagance. The grotto was an epitome of
Pope's life reflecting his changing interests and his development as a poet, beginning with his pastoral 'imaging'
as a youth in Windsor Forest. Alexis, the shepherd boy, in
the 'Summer' pastoral sought grotto retreats to 'shun the
Noonday heat'.

The grotto is one of the strongest images in classical
pastoral poetry. Originally grottoes were natural caves
with sacred springs said to be haunted by nymphs, later
artificial grottoes or architectural nymphaea were built
by the Greeks and the Romans for learned discourse and
dedicated to the Muses, the protectors of the arts and
sciences. The grotto reappears in Renaissance pastoral
poetry and in gardens. Art imitating and surpassing
nature was a potent Renaissance idea and there was no
better place than a grotto where nature's materials could
be used to advantage for garden art. The most fantastic
surviving grotto of the period is in the Boboli gardens in
Florence, recalling Alberti's words that 'the ancients used
to dress the walls of their grottoes and caverns with
all manner of rough work, with little chips of pumice'.[1]
The supreme baroque example of a grand grotto-
nyphaeum where a Sun King could recline was at
Versailles.

At Twickenham, Pope's 'Solitude and Grotto' was a
far cry from our own grotto rooms at Woburn, Wilton,
Chatsworth or Vauxhall Gardens, with their mannerist
conceits, mechanical water effects and eating facilities.
On a humbler scale were the small shell grottoes com-
mended by Addison in 1714 as fancies for 'poetical ladies',
more amusing for them than their needlework.[2] Pope
himself in his 'Lines on a Grotto at Crux-Easton, Hants'
praised the Misses Lisle who indulged in such whimsical
shell work. It needed true poetic imagination, however,
to revive the pastoral 'shadowy cave' of classical mythology in the Augustan garden.

Shaftesbury, who, with Pope and Addison was chal-
lenging the 'formal Mockery of Princely Gardens', had
already, in 1711, pointed to 'irregular unwrought Grottos'
as desirable 'Things of a *natural* kind'.[3] Evelyn, on a visit
to Cliveden in 1679 had described one natural grotto in
the chalk cliff as 'a most romantic object, and the place
altogether answers the most poetical description that can
be made of a solitude, precipice, prospects and whatever
can contribute to a thing so very like their imaginations'.[4]
Pope turned fancy into form in his own romantic artificial grotto, which was, as Homer described Calypso's
grotto, conceived as part of the landscape; 'without the
grot, a various sylvan scene,/Appears around and groves
of living green'.[5] One exit from the grotto was to the
riverside lawns, the other, through the tunnel and over-
looked by a shell temple, was to the garden.

Pope describes the first stage of his grotto-making,
the discovery of the spring, and his almost childish
delight in the atmospherics and camera obscura effects
of water and moving lights in great detail to his friend
Edward Blount in 1725:

I have put the last hand to my works of this kind, in happily finishing the subterraneous way and grotto. I there found a spring
of the clearest water, which falls in a perpetual rill, that echoes
through the cavern day and night ….It wants nothing but a
good statue with an Inscription. like that beautiful antique one
you know I am so fond of;

Huius Nympha loci, sacri custodia fontis,
Dormio, dum blandae sentio murmur aquae
Parce meum quisquis tangis Cava Marmora somnum
Rumpere Sive Bibas Sive lavere tace.

You will think that I have been very poetical in this description,
but it is pretty near the truth. I wish you were here to bear testimony how little it owes to art, either the place itself, or the
image I give of it.[6]

Homer began the tradition that Muses made their homes where fresh springs gush out of natural caverns and Pope was thrilled to find the spring when excavating the tunnel. Although he did not apparently achieve the 'nymph of the grot' which he had told Blount the place needed, the spring reinforced the idea that his grotto was a 'Musaeum', a haunt where the Muses communicated with him. When Henry Hoare constructed his romantic rock grotto by the lake at Stourhead in 1748, it appears to have been modelled on that at Twickenham; he, however, did have a nymph above his spring and used Pope's translation of the 'antique' inscription he would have liked to have used himself:

> Nymph of the grot, these sacred springs I keep
> And to the murmur of these waters sleep
> Ah spare my slumbers, gently tread the cave
> And drink in silence, or in silence lave.[7]

At Stourhead Henry Hoare had the advantage of a free-standing grotto with light brought in from the dome of the central chamber. The Twickenham grotto was in

The grotto at Stourhead. As part of the classical iconography of the garden Henry Hoare installed a sleeping nymph with Pope's inscription above the spring in the rock grotto.

the basement of the villa extended to the tunnel under the road so that light could only be obtained through camera obscura effects, 'visible radiations' on the wall through the open door or by a star-shaped 'lamp of an orbicular figure of thin alabaster' in the ceiling. A visitor from Newcastle described with great enthusiasm how Pope had used mirrors to magnify the effect of the little rill and the glittering of the spars and marbles. 'Mr Pope's poetick Genius has introduced a kind of Machinery, which performs that same Part in the Grotto that supernatural Powers and incorporeal Beings act in the heroick Species of Poetry'.[8] It all seemed more in the spirit of the magic of Aladdin's or Robinson Crusoe's caves with their myriad sparkling lights than the classical Nymphaeum, evoked by Kent in his headpiece to Pope's *Odyssey*.

The grotto at Stowe was changed to accommodate Pope's new glittering ideas in the 1740s. Gilbert West, Lord Cobham's nephew, who had much to do with Stowe, was a good friend of Pope and had sent some material for the Twickenham grotto to him from his estate at West Wickham. West went to stay with Pope for a fortnight in March 1743 and must have been impressed by the mirror effects in the grotto. In 1744 Seeley's Stowe guide records the installation of a number of looking glasses on the wall and ceiling in 'plaister work' frames set with shells and broken flints. William Gilpin, visiting Stowe in 1748 was most impressed, 'this profusion of mirrors has a very extraordinary Effect: The Place seems divided into thousand beautiful Apartments, and appears fifty times as large as it is'.[9]

Pope's grotto and garden became famous and a haunt for visitors from far and wide. The poet expressed his frustration at the outcome at the beginning of his *Epistle to Dr. Arbuthnot*:

> Shut, shut the door, good John! fatigu'd I said,
> Tye up the knocker, say I'm sick, I'm dead.
> ....
> What Walls can guard me, or what shades can hide?
> They pierce my thickets, thro' my Grot they glide,
> By land, by water, they renew the charge,
> They stop the chariot, and they board the barge.

John Serle, Pope's man-servant and gardener acted as a guide and finally, after the poet's death, when the number of visitors increased, published a 'Plan and Perspective View of the Grotto' with an 'account of all the Gems, Minerals, Spars, and Ores of which it is composed, and from whom and whence they were sent'.[10]

Over the years Pope had collected from friends at home petrifactions, ores and sparry marble; further afield there was crystal from the Hartz mines; gold ore from Peru; silver ore from Mexico; Egyptian pebbles; lava from Vesuvius; coral from the West Indies and such curios as humming birds and their nests. Joseph Spence had brought back 'a fine piece of Marble from the Grotto of Egeria' from his Grand Tour in the 1730s for his friend.[11] Spence's gift reinforced the link in Pope's mind with the idea that the Muses communicated to mortals in grottoes. In 1740 Pope wrote 'Verses on a Grotto by the River Thames at Twickenham, composed of Marbles, Spars and Minerals', which contained a special reference to the 'Aegerian grot', which now had a new meaning in the poet's life:

> Approach: But aweful! Lo! th' AEgerian *Grott*,
> Where, nobly-pensive, ST. JOHN sate and thought;
> Where British *sighs from dying* WYNDHAM *stole*
> And the bright flame was shot thro' MARCHMONT's Soul.
> Let such, such only, tread this sacred Floor,
> Who dare to love their Country, and be poor.

The poem was dedicated to Henry St John Bolingbroke, Pope's 'guide, philosopher and friend'. (Lady Hertford, who saw the poem before publication, took exception to the last two lines on the grounds that St John's poverty was due more to profligacy than patriotism). Having returned from exile and settled at his Dawley farm in 1725, the disenchanted Bolingbroke left England again in 1735, and only came back in 1738 to make arrangements to sell Dawley. He stayed with Pope for several months during which time they discussed his 'Idea for a Patriot King', in the classical republican tradition, apparently closeted in the 'Aegerian grott'. The

Kent's drawing of Pope in his grotto. Pope's grotto with its mirror and camera obscura effects was the focus of the poet's life, where he worked and communed with nature and friends.

legendary philosopher king, Numa Pompilius, had learned the art of good government through the inspiration of the nymph Egeria, who dwelt by the spring in her sacred grotto near Rome, and it was singularly felicitous that 'nobly-pensive' Bolingbroke could philosophise in the grotto in the lap of the Muses.

Bolingbroke, who was a leading contributor to *The Craftsman*, was the spearhead of the opposition to Walpole's government and tried to rally Frederick, Prince of Wales, who had severed relations with George II's court, to institute a monarchy independent of political factions which would defend the constitution against corruption and exploitation of wealth.[12] The opposition was becoming fragmented and in Pope's words 'on one alone our all relies'. George Lyttelton, the Prince of Wales's secretary, encouraged Pope to keep in contact with the prince who set great store by his advice, 'Let the Prince hear every day from the man of the Age, who is the greatest Dispenser of Fame', Lyttelton begged.[13]

The friendship progressed and in 1739 the prince sent urns for Pope's garden. He also received material from 'the prince's mine in Cornwall' for the grotto. There is an earlier recorded visit of the Prince of Wales to Pope's villa in October 1735, when, politics apart, Prince Frederick must have taken a fancy to Pope's dog Bounce, as a puppy from her next litter was sent to Kew bearing the inscription engraved on its collar:

I am His Highness' Dog at Kew;
Pray tell me Sir, whose Dog are you?

Pope acknowledged that it was Bolingbroke who had steered his course as a poet away from the descriptive pastoral poetry of 'Windsor Forest' and occasional verse, such as 'The Rape of the Lock' on to a 'series of poems which would amount to a systematic survey of human nature'. *The Essay on Man*, written in 1730, was dedicated to his mentor and the *Moral Essays* followed. Bolingbroke remained an influence on Pope all his life:

St John, whose love indulg'd my labours past
Matures my present, and shall bound my last.[14]

In his largely autobiographical *Epistle to Dr. Arbuthnot* of 1731 Pope recalls the early days before he 'moralized his song' under Bolingbroke's guidance:

Soft were my numbers; who could take offence
While pure Description held the place of Sense?
Like gentle Fanny's was my flow'ry theme,
A painted mistress, or a purling stream.[15]

These days of 'Fancy's Maze' were captured by William Kent in his romantic image of Pope in his grotto,

Sketch plan of the grotto drawn by Pope himself in December 1740.

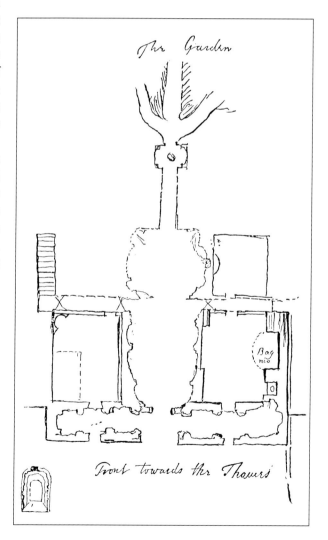

John Serle's perspective drawing of the grotto looking through to the garden from the front of the house. It shows the final stage when it had been remodelled as a mine or quarry depicting 'Nature underground' and Pope's interest in geology.

the focus of his poetic Muse; days of 'Dreams' with Swift and 'imaging' with Digby, rather than philosophising with Bolingbroke and politicians. The out-of-scale whimsical winged insects above the Muse's grotto were clearly a shared joke between Pope and his admired friend Kent. Joseph Warton saw in Pope's second pastoral the same images as in the third idyll of Theocritus and it is possible that Kent was evoking the shepherd who cries with much tenderness, 'Would I become a murmuring bee, fly into your grotto, and be permitted to creep among the leaves and ivy that compose the chaplet which adorns your head'.[16]

William Mason, like Pope a poet-gardener, wrote, in 1747, *Musaeus: A Monody to the Memory of Mr Pope* in which he made Pope die in his grotto, the epitome of his life, thereby recalling the poet's own final 'Couplet on his Grotto':

And life itself can nothing more supply
Than just to plan our projects, and to die.

The poet was mourned by Theocritus 'the Sicilian Muse', whom Pope had transferred to 'blest Thames shores', with the shades of Chaucer, Spenser and Milton standing by (see page 128). Milton praises him for 'countless graces', but particularly his grotto. Mason linked Pope's self-effacing comments to Dr Arbuthnot on his early poetry, 'That not in Fancy's Maze he wander'd long,/ But stoop'd to Truth, and moraliz'd his song',[17] with the idea that his grotto, in which the Monody is set, was a poet's fanciful 'plaything'; in Mason's words:

the toys of thoughtless youth,
When flow'ry fiction held the place of truth
When fancy rul'd.[18]

Pope's 'grottofying' had in fact gone through the same phases as his verse; the grotto, in which Mason envisaged the poet dying, was rather different from that sketched by Kent in 1725, when 'fancy ruled'. Pope had written to Bolingbroke, back in France, in September 1740 to describe his later ideas:

Next to patching up my Constitution, my great Business has been to patch up a Grotto (the same you have so often sate in the sunny part under my house) with all the varieties of nature under ground, spars, minerals and marbles. I hope yet to live to philosophise with you in this museum, which is now a study for virtuosi, and a scene for contemplation.[19]

The following month he wrote to Dr Oliver, his physician friend in Bath, where he had been 'patching up my Constitution', that the grotto was 'my present pride and pleasure', confiding that 'I am so fond of it, that I should be more sorry to leave it unfinished, than any other work I can at present think of '.[20] Pope had first spent some weeks in Bristol taking the waters at Hotwells Spa in the Avon gorge, where he was deeply impressed by the great variety of colours in the rocky cliffs. He described to Martha Blount how, looking out of the door of the house, he saw 'a vast Rock of 100 foot high, of red, white, green, blue and yellowish Marbles, all botch'd and variegated'.[21]

A detail of Kent's drawing of Pope's garden (see page 64) showing the entrance to the grotto from the garden side and the Thames beyond seen through the Shell temple.

Kent's shell temples outside the grotto at Stowe closely resembled Pope's garden temple.

When Pope moved on to Bath he stayed at Widcombe with Ralph Allen, who was building his monumental Prior Park. While there he gave advice to Allen's wife on the making of her grotto and in 1740 wrote to her that he rejoiced that she had 'begun to imitate the Great Works of nature, rather than the Baubles most ladies affect'.[22] Her grotto, where the Allens later buried the Great Dane puppy, another offspring of Pope's dog Bounce, has just been discovered by the National Trust. There was no lack of material to hand for the grotto as Allen was working the Bath stone mines on Combe Down, which had made him a rich man in the building of Bath. Pope was fascinated by nature manipulated by man's industry underground in Allen's quarries and began to see new possibilities for his grotto. He particularly admired the pillar and stall structure, whereby rough hewn pillars were left standing to support the roof.[23]

The man who would help Pope with his geological aspirations to adorn his subterranean grotto was Dr Oliver's kinsman, the Revd William Borlase of Ludgvan, who wrote *The Natural History of Cornwall*. Borlase was a great authority on deep Cornish tin mining and Pope learned from him how the metal lodes occurred in east-west veins and how the materials were layered.[24] At Dr Oliver's request Borlase sent by tinship to London and up the Thames by barge to Pope's Twickenham grotto 'three or four Tun, of the finest Spar, Mundick, Copper and Tin Oars, which you shall judge proper for such a work'.[25] Pope made a new Borlase room, assisted by one of Allen's masons, with the Cornish materials laid out in their natural strata and in the same orientation. Pope told Allen that he hoped that the experts would think that he had 'imitated nature well'.[26] At this time Spence returned from his 1742 Grand Tour and offered Pope 'some beads and medals that had been blessed at Loreto' for his grotto, but these were politely refused.[27]

Pope's grotto was unique in its combination of the Musaeum, a seat of the Muses of Greek mythology, and its successor the museum, a collection of rarities – the sense in which Pope used the word when referring to 'this museum, which is now a study for virtuosi' in his letter to Bolingbroke.[28] Many seventeenth-century gentlemen had 'cabinets of curiosities' in their houses or as garden rooms and galleries and in Pope's day the most famous was that of Sir Hans Sloane at Chelsea. Pope was delighted when the great virtuoso presented him with some joints from the basaltic columns of the Giant's Causeway in Ireland.

Pope's achievement was to present nature's geological curiosities, not in a building, but authentically in an underground grotto setting where he could invite visitors to 'Approach. Great Nature studiously behold' which was all the more 'aweful' as being the 'sacred Floor' where, 'nobly-pensive, St. John sate and thought'. By linking scientific, classical and romantic nature, Pope's grotto was a seminal event in the eighteenth-century search to establish man's relationship with nature.

Kent's headpiece to volume five of Pope's *Odyssey*. Calypso's grotto, where Odysseus was entertained by the nymph for seven years, resembles the structure of Pope's grotto as seen in the perspective view.

1. Alberti, Leon Battista, *De re aedificatoria*, 1485, 9.4
2. Addison, *The Spectator*, no.632, 1714.
3. see Chapter 1, note 21.
4. *The Diary of John Evelyn*, ed. E.S. de Beer, 1855, vol.IV, p.177.
5. *Odyssey*, Book V, l.80.
6. *Correspondence*, 2:296-97.
7. The Latin inscription given above (page 55) was found in many Renaissance garden grottoes.
8. 'An Epistolary Description of the Late Mr. Pope's House and Gardens at Twickenham', *The General Magazine* of Newcastle, January 1748; published in *The Genius of the Place*, ed. John Dixon Hunt and Peter Willis, 1975.
9. William Gilpin, *A Dialogue upon the Gardens at Stow*, 1748.
10. For a full account of the materials see Anthony Beckles Willson, *Alexander Pope's Grotto in Twickenham*, 1998.
11. Joseph Spence, *Letters from the Grand Tour*, ed. Slava Klima, 1975. For Pope see pp.22, 109, 114, 377.
12. *The Craftsman*, to which Bolingbroke contributed, was started in 1726; Sir Robert Walpole was 'the man of craft'.
13. *Correspondence*, 4:139.
14. *Imitations of Horace*, Epistle I, Book I, ll.1-2.
15. ll.147-50.
16. Joseph Warton, *Essay on the Writings and Genius of Pope*, 1756, vol.I, p.8.
17. ll.340-41
18. W.Mason, 'Musaeus, A Monody to the Memory of Mr. Pope', 1747, p.11.
19. *Correspondence*, 4:262.
20. *Correspondence*, 4:279.
21. *Correspondence*, 4:201.
22. *Correspondence*, 4:254.
23. *Correspondence*, 4:246.
24. Ibid.
25. For Oliver-Borlase correspondence see Benjamin Boyce, 'Mr Pope, in Bath, improves the Design of his Grotto' in *Restoration and 18th century Literature*, ed. Carroll Camden, 1963, pp.146-47.
26. *Correspondence*, 4:254.
27. Spence, *Observations*, no.353.
28. *Correspondence*, 4:262.

'GARDENING IS NEAR-AKIN TO PHILOSOPHY'

William Kent's drawing of Pope's garden at Twickenham:
a classical scene with gods at the end of a rainbow, complete with
sacrificial altar, antique tripod and bust of Homer. 'Descending
Gods have found Elysium here'. Kent has his arm round Pope
and Bounce is much in evidence.

KNOW, *all the distant Din that World can keep*
Rolls o'er my Grotto, *and but sooths my Sleep.*
There, my Retreat the best Companions grace,
Chiefs, out of War, and Statesmen, out of Place.
There St. John mingles with my friendly Bowl,
The Feast of Reason and the Flow of Soul:
And He, whose Lightning pierc'd th'Iberian Lines,
Now, forms my Quincunx, and now ranks my Vines,
Or tames the Genius of the stubborn Plain,
Almost as quickly, as he conquer'd Spain.

Alexander Pope: *Imitations of Horace, Book II, Satire I,*
To Mr. Fortescue, lines 123–32.

THE VISITOR'S INTRODUCTION TO POPE'S garden was through the grotto, which even Borlase, who appreciated 'all the delicacies of subterraneous nature' to be found there, recognised was only a preparation 'into the Elyzium it lead him to'.[1] In contrast to the more architectural undercroft entrance to the grotto forming part of the villa, the exit porch from the underground grotto passage was more romantic, consisting in John Serle's words of 'various sorts of Stones thrown promiscuously together, in imitation of an old Ruine; some full of Holes, others like Honeycombs' which came from Ralph Allen's Bath quarries.

A cockle-shell path led from the grotto through an arcade of trees, bordered by wilderness groves, to a shell temple open on all sides to the garden. Looking back through the 'sloping Arcade of Trees' and the tunnel, Pope tells us that you could 'see the Sails on the River passing suddenly and vanishing, as thro' a Perspective Glass',[2] as seen in William Kent's drawing. The oblique nature of the design immediately struck the visitor, being different from the usual entrance to a garden designed to be seen from a terrace or from the windows of a house. The elongated central compartments were enclosed by irregular plantations through which walks were contrived, some meandering and some straight; from the orangery they radiated out in the old-fashioned goose-foot manner.

The mount, immediately in front of the shell temple, had probably been made from the spoil dug from the tunnel under the road; it was essential to the garden, which was shut off from the river landscape by the house. By 1721 Pope was being instructed how to slide down it by some young Twickenham friends, but more sedate visitors, such as Voltaire, were taken up 'to shew you the glory of my kingdom'. There was a seat on top and it was from here that the great Frenchman admired the Thames landscape looking towards Richmond Hill. The layout of the poet's garden was particularly enjoyed by visitors as seen from the mount overlooking the shell temple, and 'the various Distribution of the Thickets, Grass plots, Alleys, Banks &c', and they could also watch a game of bowls on his green.[3]

Lord Bathurst, Pope's 'large-acred' friend of Cirencester Park, joked about the Lilliputian garden and its diminutive owner. He threatened to 'send one of my wood-Carts and bring away your whole house and Gardens, and stick it in the middle of Oakley-wood where it will never be heard of any more, unless some of the children find it in Nutting-season and take possession of it thinking I have made it for them'.[4] Pope had no illusions about his activities and told Lord Strafford, 'I am busy in three inches of gardening as any man can be in threescore acres. I fancy myself like the fellow that spent his life in cutting ye twelve apostles in one cherry stone. I have a Theatre, an Arcade, a Bowling-green, a Grove, and what not'.[5]

Nevertheless, as with his grotto, Pope was constantly changing his garden, which, he said, 'like my Life, seems to me every Year to want Correction and require alteration'.[6] His garden meant a great deal to him, especially as his frailty increased. A year before his death he wrote to a friend, 'I have lived much by myself of late…partly to amuse myself with little improvements in my garden and house, to which possibly (if I live) I may soon be more confined'.[7]

John Serle said that when his master took over there were 'not ten sticks in the garden'. What delighted Pope was the practical contact with organic nature experienced by a gardener through horticulture; a practical way of showing his own responses to the natural order of the world, akin to natural philosophy. 'Nature shall join you; Time shall make it grow'. The year after he began his garden he was writing, 'Our gardens are offering their first Nosegays; our Trees, like new Acquaintance brought happily together are stretching their Arms to meet each other and growing nearer and nearer every Hour. The

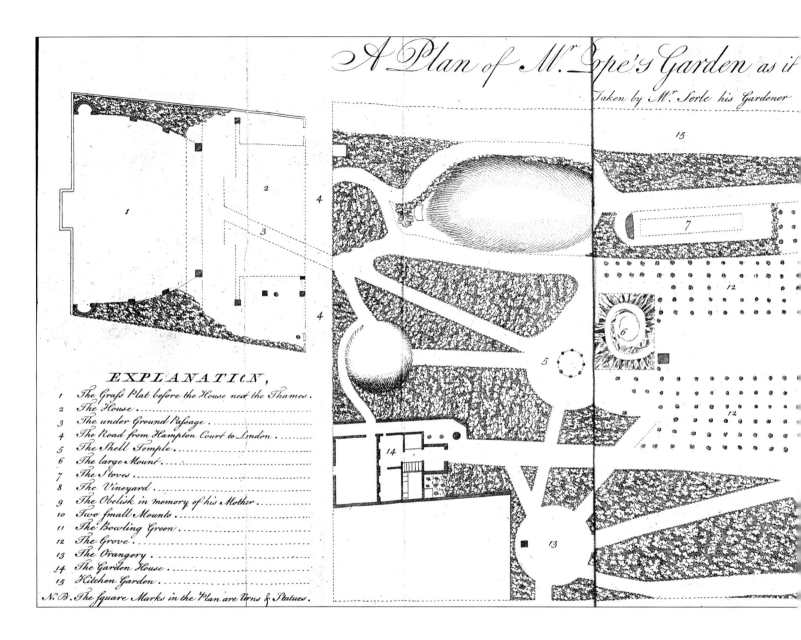

A Plan of Mr Pope's Garden as it

Taken by Mr Serle his Gardener

EXPLANATION,

1   The Grass Plat before the House next the Thames.
2   The House.
3   The under Ground Passage.
4   The Road from Hampton Court to London.
5   The Shell Temple.
6   The large Mount.
7   The Stoves.
8   The Vineyard.
9   The Obelisk in memory of his Mother.
10   Two small Mounts.
11   The Bowling Green.
12   The Grove.
13   The Orangery.
14   The Garden House.
15   Kitchen Garden.

N.B. The Square Marks in the Plan are Urns & Statues.

Birds are paying their thanksgiving Songs for the new Habitations I have made 'em'.[8]

In February 1723 Gay told Swift that the poet 'of late …has talk'd only as a Gardiner', and Pope once said to Ralph Allen, 'I thank God for every Wet day and for every Fog, that gives me the headake, but prospers my works'.[9]

In the summer of 1723 Digby was asking, 'How thrive your garden plants? how look the trees? how spring the Brocoli and Fenochio? hard names to spell! how did the poppies bloom?'[10] In due course Pope was able to take plants to his friends on his visits; and they apparently prospered as Aaron Hill could say in 1738, 'I stole the

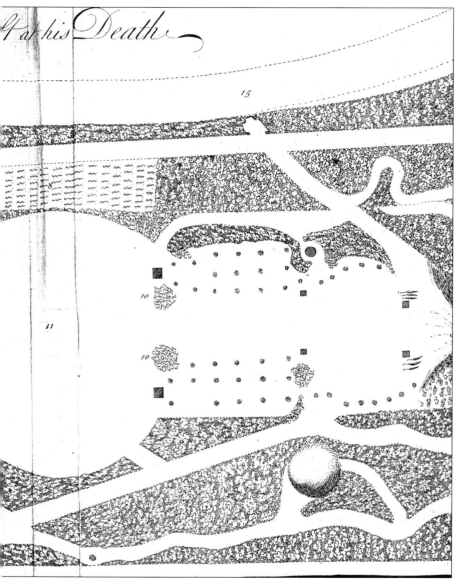

of at his Death

John Serle's plan of Pope's garden from his guidebook which included a perspective view of the grotto, an inventory of its materials and an anthology of verses on the grotto. Pope's garden was very influential in terms of 'pleasing intracacies' in the layout but it needed Kent to advance the poet's visionary theories as set out in 'Consult the Genius of the Place'.

delight of conversing, great part of a day, with some vegetable children of yours'.[11]

There were many good nurseries and gardeners in the area. Batty Langley and perhaps his father Daniel rented land close to hand in Cross Deep and, if they used the land for nurseries as well as produce, Pope's highly regarded weeping willows by the river may well have come from them. Batty Langley was gardener at Twickenham Park for Thomas Vernon, who was Pope's landlord. Vernon was a Turkey merchant and was said to have introduced the weeping willow into England. Batty Langley reported that they were flourishing in Twickenham Park in the 1720s. There were many gardening experts settled by the Thames; James Johnston of Twickenham, Sir Henry Capel at Kew, Sir Matthew Decker of Richmond, famous for his pineapples, and Walpole's highly-regarded 'treemonger', Lord Ilay at Whitton.[12]

One expert particularly involved with Pope's garden was his friend Lord Peterborough, who had a renowned botanical garden and orchard at his home at Parson's Green, Fulham. In the Satire 'To Mr. Fortescue', Pope refers to Lord Peterborough, who 'Now, forms my Quincunx, and now ranks my Vines'. Cicero's plantations were said to have been laid out in the quincunx order. Serle's plan of Pope's two quincunx groves shows squares rather than the five tree domino formation of the classical quincunx, but John James had pointed out in his widely-read *The Theory and Practice of Gardening* in 1712, dedicated to James Johnston, that squares would have the same effect if the trees were set very exactly with no hedges or palisades erected between them.

Professional help for Pope's garden came from Charles Bridgeman, whom he had probably first met at the Princess of Wales's gardening conference in 1719.[13] They had mutual friendships with Matthew Prior and James Gibbs and Pope knew and admired Bridgeman's work at Richmond, Stowe and Wimpole. Bridgeman was a subscriber to Pope's *Odyssey* and Pope considered him 'of the Virtuosi-Class as well as I ...and in My notions, of the higher kind of class, since Gardening is more Antique

The view down to St Mary's, Twickenham, as it is today from the riverbank beside what was Pope's lawn. The villa, garden and grotto acted like a magnet. Pope had visits from Voltaire, Swift, Gay, Prince Frederick and Bolingbroke.

Below. Bridgeman's amphitheatre at Claremont from a contemporary painting. Bridgeman, a past master at earthworks, made a miniature 'Bridgmannick theatre' for Pope at Twickenham.

and nearer God's own Work than Poetry'.[14] Bridgeman's speciality was in earthworks and now that his amphitheatre at Claremont has been restored one of his best achievements can once more be seen. Pope's 'Bridgmannick Theatre', carried out in 1726 was minute by comparison.

An innovation in gardening was the way in which Pope used the art of creating perspective and optical illusion, which he had learned from the painter Charles Jervas, to give greater distance to his short alleys. 'You may distance things by darkening them and by narrowing the plantation more and more toward the end, in the same manner as they do in painting', he told Spence.[15] Pope's gardener must have discussed this with Batty Langley, who in his *New Principles of Gardening* in 1728 recommends that the 'Walks leading up the slopes of a Mount have their Breadth contracted at the Top, full one half part; and if the contracted Part be enclosed on the Sides with a Hedge whose leaves are of a light Green 'twill

seemingly add a great Addition to the Length of the Walk, when view'd from the other End'.

Pope also worked out the psychology of emotional associations in relation to visual effect, inducing melancholy or cheerful moods by various planting. After his mother's death in 1733, he erected an obelisk in her memory at the end of a solemn cypress walk. Horace Walpole recorded that 'the passing through the gloom from the grotto to the opening day, the retiring and again assembling shades, the dusky groves, the larger lawn, and the solemnity of the termination at the cypresses that lead up to his mother's tomb, are managed with exquisite judgement'.[16]

Walpole made reference to the theatrical element of Pope's garden. 'It was a singular effort of art and taste to impress so much variety and scenery on a spot of five acres'. Scenery, in the pre-Gilpin era referred to stage scenery and Walpole commented on the 'two or three little lawns opening and opening beyond one another' to

J.C.Buckler's drawing of the obelisk and urns, designed by Kent in 1738, and erected by Pope in memory of his mother. The photograph shows them today in the grounds of Penn House, Amersham, Bucks.

entice the eye as through stage effects. Another visitor, Elizabeth Carter, referred to 'broken views' from the Mount and 'discovering' vistas to the Thames. In 1738 she astutely commented that Pope's garden 'if not so unbounded as his Genius has as much variety in it'.[17]

Walpole saw Pope's garden as related to his poetry as Spence had done. The garden had matured into a miniature Windsor Forest when Walpole saw it; he felt that it looked as though it was 'surrounded with thick inpenetrable woods' as some of the later views from the river

depict it. The visitor from Newcastle, who in 1747 described the grotto in such detail, writes equally enthusiastically on Pope's garden as an 'elegant Retreat of a Poet strongly inspired with the Love of Nature and Retirement'. As no 'Shear-work' was permitted even the regular parts, shown on Serle's plan, appear natural as intended:

The Middel of the Garden approaches nearest to a Lawn or open Green, but is delightfully diversified with Banks and

Hillocks; which are entirely cover'd with Thickets of Lawrel, Bay, Holly and many other Evergreens and Shrubs, rising one above another in beautiful Slopes and Inter-mixtures, where Nature freely lays forth the Branches, and disports uncontrul'd; except what may be entirely prun'd away for more Decency and Convenience to the surrounding Grass-plots.[18]

Most of what we know about Pope's garden theory comes from his fellow garden-philosopher and designer Joseph Spence.[19] From 1726 Spence recorded conversations with Pope and other literary figures; although not published until 1820 as his *Anecdotes* (and more recently as his *Observations*), these were widely known and quoted and made available to Warburton and Johnson for their biographical comments. Spence's own life of Pope was never written. He met Pope first at the poet's request after he published 'An Essay on Pope's Odyssey in which some particular Beauties and Blemishes are considered' in 1726. After an amicable meeting Spence said, 'I'm in love with Mr. Pope: he has the most generous Spirit in the World'.[20] They remained close friends for the rest of Pope's life, Spence attending him at his final illness.

Spence was often abroad as bear-leader on young noblemen's grand tours, and it was on one of these occasions he brought back some marble fragments from the Egerian grotto for Pope. He observed in 1732 that 'Mr Pope was talked of in Italy almost with more applause than here among us', and that people were learning English in order to read him.[21] Spence basked in the reflected glory of his critical study of the *Odyssey*. In spite of his frequent travelling, Spence stayed with Pope about four times a year and the poet visited him in Oxford when he became Professor of Poetry in 1728.

Spence was also a classical scholar and at Oxford and during his visits to Italy be began to collect material for his *Polymetis*, a work which related classical literature and art; it was very popular but not finally published until 1747. It would certainly have been discussed with Pope, whose lines featured on the title-page:

The verse and sculpture bore an equal part,
And Art reflected images to Art.[22]

Polymetis's dialogues took place in a landscape garden, 'rather wild than regular' and like Stowe it had a profusion of temples.

The final step in Pope's garden-making was to have been classical statuary by the Thames. In 1743, the year

Joseph Spence (1699-1768), Pope's Boswell, recorded conversations with him and other literary figures from 1726. These were widely known and quoted and used by Warburton and Johnson for their biographies. As a fellow gardener/philosopher he revealed much of Pope's garden theory and later as a garden designer copied much from Twickenham.

before Pope died, Spence reported a conversation in which he said, 'Why I really shall be at loss for the diversion I used to take in laying out and finishing things and I have now nothing left for me to do but to add a little ornament or two at the line to the Thames'.[23] Spence went on to say, 'his design for this was to have a swan, as flying into the river, on each side of the landing place, then the statues of two river gods reclined on the bank between them'. The classical imagery of the river gods was discussed with Spence and it was clearly of the greatest importance that the inscriptions should relate appropriately and that the river gods should enhance the

Thames scene. Further downstream Pope felt nothing but contempt for the 'two miserable little leaden figures of a dog and bitch' that James Johnston had placed, unsuitably, on his wall by the river in the Arcadian Thames.[24]

Walpole, who went to live in Twickenham three years after Pope's death, used to take visitors to Strawberry Hill across the road to the poet's garden. Walpole greatly regretted the way Pope's successor had later 'hacked and hewed' the 'sacred groves'. He had relished his 'little perspective' garden and the little compartments the poet had 'twisted and twirled and rhymed and harmonized' as intricately and painstakingly as his verses; they were now so opened up and exposed that 'if the Muses wanted to tie up their garters there is not a nook to do it in without being seen'.[25]

It was the variety and 'pleasing intricacies' of Pope's garden, managed, as Walpole said, with such 'art and deception' that appealed to visitors in the 1720s, who were used to the square formal walled gardens, seen at nearby Ham and Hampton Court and in Kip engravings, and scathingly described by Pope:

> No pleasing Intricacies intervene,
> No artful wildness to perplex the Scene;
> Grove nods at Grove, each Alley has a brother,
> And half the platform just reflects the other.[26]

William Gilpin, the pioneer of the Picturesque, affirmed that Pope's garden was very influential as it was:

surprizing to see such an effect of real taste, at a time when the country was barbarous in all its ideas of gardening.... Pope certainly assumed to himself the merit of forming this piece of ground and used to say, with perhaps some little degree of affectation, that of all his works he valued himself most on his garden.[27]

1. Borlase correspondence quoted in Benjamin Boyce, 'Pope Improves his Grotto', *Restoration and 18th century Literature*, ed. Carroll Camden, 1963.
2. *Correspondence*, 2:296.
3. Letter in *The General Magazine* of Newcastle, see *The Genius of the Place*, p.252.
4. *Correspondence*, 3:134.
5. *Correspondence*, 2:328.
6. *Correspondence*, 4:40.
7. *Correspondence*, 4:448.
8. *Correspondence*, 2:44.
9. *Correspondence*, 4:40.
10. *Correspondence*, 2:192.
11. *Correspondence*, 4:94
12. See Ray Desmond, *Blest Retreats*, 1984, for Richmond and Twickenham gardeners.
13. *Correspondence*, 2:14.
14. *Correspondence*, 2:264.
15. Spence, *Observations*, no.610.
16. Horace Walpole, 'On Modern Gardening' in *Anecdotes of Painting*, ed. Dallaway, 1827, vol.4, p.268. The vases are illustrated in J. Vardy, *Some Designs of Mr Inigo Jones and Mr William Kent*, 1744.
17. G. Hampshire, 'Johnson, Elizabeth Carter and Pope's garden', *Notes and Queries*, 217, June 1972, p.221.
18. Letter in *The General Magazine* of Newcastle, *op. cit.* p.251.
19. For Joseph Spence and his gardening see R.W.King 'Joseph Spence of Byfleet', *Garden History*, vols 6, no.3 (1978) pp.38-64; 7, no.3 (1979), pp.29-48; 8, no.2 (1980), pp.44-65.
20. Spence, vol.1, xxiv-v.
21. Joseph Spence, *Letters from the Grand Tour*, ed. Slava Klima, p.88.
22. *Epistle: To Mr. Addison*, ll.51-52.
23. Spence, *Observations*, no.620.
24. *The Twickenham Edition of the Poems of Alexander Pope*, ed. John Butt, vol.VI, p.45. Pope disliked Secretary Johnston's taste in politics and literature but his only comment on his horticulturally 'curious' famous garden was to condemn his riverside statues.
25. *Correspondence of Horace Walpole*, ed. W.S.Lewis, 1937-83. The desecration of Pope's garden is reported in vol. 25: 177.
26. *Epistle IV: To Richard Boyle, Earl of Burlington*, ll.115-18.
27. William Gilpin, *Tour of the Highlands*, vol.II, 1789 (tour made 1776), p.192.

'VILLAS OF THE ANCIENTS' — MARBLE HILL

The Countess of Suffolk's House at Twickenham, engraving by James Mason after Augustin Heckel, 1749. Marble Hill remains a little Palladian gem to be seen from the river, giving the Thames an air of the River Brenta.

In Spight of *Pope*, in Spight of *Gay*,
And all that He or They can say;
Sing on I must, and sing I will
Of *Richmond*-Lodge, and *Marble*-Hill.

LAST *Friday* Night, as Neighbours use,
This Couple met to talk of News.
For by old Proverbs it appears,
That Walls have Tongues and Hedges, Ears.

Marble-Hill

Quoth *Marble-Hill*, right well I ween,
Your Mistress now is grown a Queen;
You'll find it soon by woful Proof,
She'll come no more beneath your Roof.

Richmond-Lodge

The kingly Prophet well evinces,
That we should put no Trust in Princes;
My Royal Master promis'd me
To raise me to a high Degree:
But now He's grown a King, God wot,
I fear I shall be soon forgot.
You see, when Folks have got their Ends,
How quickly they neglect their Friends;
Yet I may say 'twixt me and you,
Pray God they now may find as true.

Marble-Hill

My House was built but for a Show,
My Lady's empty Pockets know:
And now she will not have a Shilling
To raise the Stairs, or build the Cieling;
For, all the Courtly Madams round,
Now pay four Shillings in the Pound.
'Tis come to what I always thought;
My Dame is hardly worth a Groat.
Had You and I been Courtiers born,
We should not thus have layn forlorn;
For, those we dext'rous Courtiers call,
Can *rise* upon their Master's *Fall*.
But, we unlucky and unwise,
Must *fall*, because our Masters *rise*.

Richmond-Lodge

My Master scarce a Fortnight since,
Was grown as wealthy as a Prince;
But now it will be no such thing,
For he'll be poor as any *King*;
And, by his Crown will nothing get;
But, like a King, to run in Debt.

Marble-Hill

No more the Dean, that grave Divine,
Shall keep the Key of my (no) Wine;
My Ice-house rob as heretofore,
And steal my Artichokes no more;
Poor *Patty Blount* no more be seen
Bedraggled in my Walks so green:
Plump *Johnny Gay* will now elope;
And here no more will dangle *Pope*.

Richmond-Lodge

Here wont the *Dean* when he's to seek,
To spunge a Breakfast once a Week;
To cry the Bread was stale, and mutter
Complaints against the Royal Butter,
But, now I fear it will be said,
No Butter sticks upon his Bread.
We soon shall find him full of Spleen,
For want of tattling to the Queen;
Stunning her Royal Ears with talking;
His *Rev'rence* and her *Highness* walking:
Whilst Lady *Charlotte*, like a Stroller,
Sits mounted on the Garden Roller,
A goodly Sight to see her ride,
With antient *Mirmont* at her Side.
In Velvet Cap his Head lies warm;
His Hat for Show, beneath his Arm.

Marble-Hill

Some *South Sea* Broker from the City,
Will purchase me, the more's the Pity,
Lay all my fine Plantations waste,
To fit them to his Vulgar Taste;
Chang'd for the worse in ev'ry Part
My Master *Pope* will break his Heart.

Richmond-Lodge

In my own *Thames* may I be drownded,
If e'er I stoop beneath a crown'd Head:
Except her Majesty prevails
To place me with the Prince of *Wales*.
And then I shall be free from Fears,
For, he'll be Prince these fifty Years.
I then will turn a Courtier too,
And serve the Times as others do.
Plain loyalty not built on Hope,
I leave to your Contriver, *Pope*:
None loves his King and Country better,
Yet none was ever less their Debtor.

Marble-Hill

Then, let him come and take a Nap,
In *Summer*, on my verdant Lap:
Prefer our *Villaes* where the *Thames* is,
To *Kensington*, or hot St. *James*'s;
Nor shall I dull in Silence sit;
For, 'tis to me he owes his Wit;
My Groves, my Ecchoes, and my Birds,
Have taught him his poetick Words.
We Gardens, and you Wildernesses,
Assist all Poets in Distresses,
Him twice a Week I here expect,
To rattle *Moody* for Neglect;
An idle Rogue, who spends his Quartridge
In tipling at the *Dog* and *Partridge*;
And I can hardly get him down
Three times a Week to brush my Gown.

Richmond-Lodge

I pity you, dear *Marble-Hill*;
But, hope to see you flourish still.
All Happiness - and so adieu.

Marble-Hill

Kind *Richmond-Lodge*; the same to you.

Jonathan Swift, 'A Pastoral Dialogue
between Richmond-Lodge and Marble-Hill'. Written
June 1727, just after the news of the king's death.

MARBLE HILL WAS THE HAPPIEST OF Pope's 'Twitnam's bowers' in the Arcadian life he created for himself. He had already paid mock court to Henrietta Howard, the Chloe of his Eclogues, at her Woman of the Bedchamber lodgings at Richmond before the Prince of Wales advanced her the money to build herself a villa at Twickenham in 1724. Amateur architects and gardening lords flocked to her assistance once the lease was negotiated with Pope's own landlord, Vernon, who was a major landowner in Twickenham. Lord Herbert took charge of the building arrangements and the elderly Peterborough fancied himself in the role of her 'gallant Gardiner'.[1] Lord Bathurst sent lambs from nearby Riskins for Pope's 'Pastoral Lady' and Lord Ilay, who was one of the trustees appointed by the prince to take care of her allowance, gave expert arboricultural advice and sent his gardener, Daniel Crofts, to assist with the planting. A huge black walnut tree from his Whitton nursery can still be seen.

Marble Hill was to be as important architecturally as Chiswick and remains a little Palladian gem to be seen from the river, giving the Thames an air of the River Brenta. Unlike Lord Burlington's villa it was designed as a residence and not simply a cultural adjunct to the main house. The owner was herself a connoisseur but also a lady intending to live on her own with an eye for comfort and propriety as well as Palladian elegance. Pope's 'reasonable Woman' had no wish to 'starve by rules of art' with winds whistling through long arcades and took care to supervise the plans that Lord Herbert drew up with Roger Morris. Nevertheless the villa's classical purity must have impressed even Lord Burlington, the great arbiter of taste. The hall was modelled on Palladio's interpretation of the atrium of a Roman house as described by Vitruvius, and Pope wrote in 1727 in her absence to say that he and Gay thought it 'the most delightful room in the world except where you are'.[2]

Pope was, according to Swift in his introduction to his 'A Pastoral Dialogue between Richmond-Lodge and Marble-Hill' (see page opposite), written in 1727, the 'contriver' of the gardens at Marble Hill. It was unclear how this should be interpreted as it was known that Charles Bridgeman was also involved; however, two undated new plans have recently come to light in the Hobart papers in the Norfolk Record Office which may throw some light on Swift's claim. The first plan, attributed to Pope, was never implemented but the second seems to be a survey and probably shows the later Marble Hill layout as carried out.

Pope's letters indicate that he did produce a plan for the gardens in 1724. He had been with Digby at Sherborne in the summer and when he wrote to Martha Blount he asked her to tell Henrietta Howard that he had spent many hours 'in drawing new plans for her'.[3] He was still engaged in his *Odyssey* translation and in September wrote to tell his collaborator, William Broome, that he was 'very busy in laying out of a garden', but was proceeding with the fourteenth book.[4]

As we have seen, Pope probably met Charles Bridgeman as early as 1719 and had come to respect him as 'of the Virtuosi-Class as well as I'.[5] He knew personally of his competence as a surveyor and in laying out ground and it would be natural for him to seek Bridgeman's professional help over his plan for Marble Hill on site; this had taken place by the end of the month as a letter from Bridgeman to Pope, dated 28 September 1724, told him that he had been very busy since meeting the poet and Mrs Howard there but was working on the 'plann'. He asked Pope to meet him in town 'that I may a little explain to you, or if not I will Send it to You by my man on Wednesday morning'.[6]

A possible explanation for the origin of the unsigned plan is that it was first sketched by Pope but the draughtsmanship and measurements were worked up by Bridgeman, who had already surveyed the ground with him. The design could not have been by Bridgeman, but

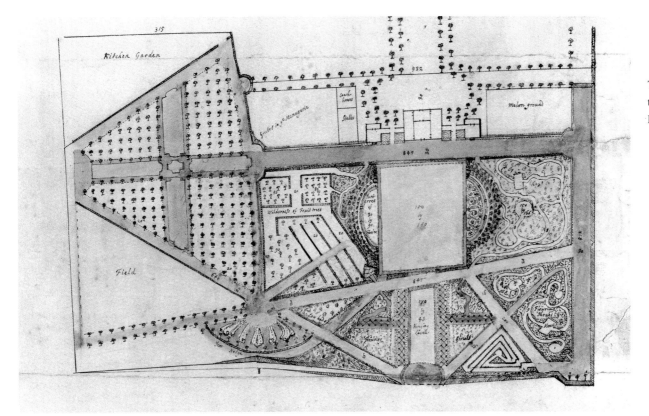

on the other hand Pope could not have undertaken a professional plan of that nature. The plan may have all the 'variety' and absence of repetition advocated by Pope, but it has none of Bridgeman's professional unity of design.

Rough garden sketches, presumably ideas for Marble Hill were discovered sketched on the backs of Pope's letters in his *Odyssey* papers in the British Library.[7] These intriguing contrivances in which twisted but not serpentined paths carve out mazy bowers and alcoves must surely be what Swift called 'tramgams' (the teasing expression possibly deriving from *trames*, the Latin for a path), when he later told Pope, after returning to Ireland, that to regain his health he should 'contrive new tramgams in your garden, or in Mrs Howard's, or my Lord Bolingbroke's'.[8]

The 'plann' of 1724 seems rather contrary as a design by someone who in the garden essay in *The Guardian* had maintained that 'all Art consists in the Imitation and Study of Nature'; it does, however, tie up with Pope's neighbour, Batty Langley's ideas on the 'arti-natural' style, which he first set out in his *Practical Geometry* of 1726 and expanded and illustrated in his *New Principles of Gardening* in 1728. Following Addison and Pope, Langley condemns those 'who deviate from Nature instead of imitating it' and calls for 'delightful meanders' instead of 'a stiff regular garden'. This was only symbolic nature, however, leading to 'false extremes' as William Mason pointed out in his exposition on *The English Garden* and had nothing to do with the wide province of nature that Kent and Brown would imitate.[9]

Pope does not name Batty Langley in his letters nor is he mentioned in the anecdotes of his gardening confidant, Joseph Spence, but the author of *New Principles of Gardening* was well acquainted with Pope's own garden where in the early twenties the first break from regular gardening with tentative meandering could be seen. Langley certainly took ideas from Pope on perspective planting. He may also have known about Pope's proposals for Marble Hill as he was working at the neighbouring

garden of James Johnston, now Orleans House, where in 1728 he made suggestions for 'arti-natural' improvements to the old fashioned garden, which he illustrated as Plate IX in his book.[10]

Clearly Swift thought that the Marble Hill garden was still in the making when he wrote his letter in 1731. In the summer of 1725, the year after the plan had been drawn up, when Pope stayed at Stowe, admiring Bridgeman's work, he was already thinking of modifications as he did constantly for his own garden. Henrietta Howard was told by Martha Blount that 'he is come back very full of plans for buildings and gardens which I find is not so much to the beautys of Lord Cobham's as the desire he has of being serviceable to you at Marble Hill'.[11]

However, the next summer when Pope, Swift and Gay were enjoying visiting Marble Hill during Henrietta's absence at court, we hear little about gardening activities except their drinking the health of a new calf, listening to birdsong in the wilderness and the kitchen garden producing a 'lettice of the Greek island called Cos'.[12] This period, 1726-27, when the villa, at least on the ground floor, was first ready for occupation, saw a special bond between Pope, Gay and Swift. John Gay, whose patron, the Duchess of Queensberry, lived across the river, was writing his *Fables*, illustrated by Kent (see page 100), and Swift was preoccupied with publishing his *Gulliver's Travels*. Pope, encouraged by Swift, had embarked on his mock-heroic satire, *The Dunciad*. Bolingbroke called the powerful literary trio, who were the leading lights of the old Scriblerus Club formed to ridicule false taste, the 'three Yahoos of Twickenham'. Martha (Patty) Blount, whose friendship with Henrietta Howard Pope had encouraged, was then living at Petersham.

Henrietta Howard was always short of money and 1727 was an anxious year for her. The Prince of Wales became George II and her services were now required at Kensington and other royal palaces as well. Richmond Lodge was given to Queen Caroline personally and so she was also in attendance there, but there was some fear that now the royal benefactor had become king he might

Plate IX from Batty Langley's *New Principles of Gardening*, 1728, showing a proposed layout in the arti-natural style for James Johnston's garden (now Orleans House) next to Marble Hill.

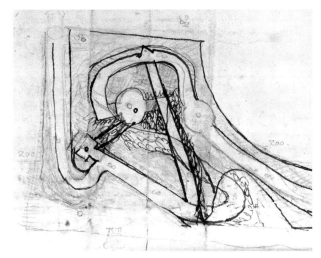

One of Pope's 'tramgams'. These little sketches of garden plans were found among his manuscript translations of Homer.

withdraw his financial support for Marble Hill. Before he returned to Ireland in 1727, Dean Swift wrote his 'Pastoral Dialogue between Richmond-Lodge and Marble-Hill' expressing the fears that he and his friends might soon have to forgo the delights of Mrs Howard's villa, where he was in charge of the wine cellar.

The royal support was not in fact withdrawn but could not be counted on and work still had to proceed slowly, especially as there was difficulty with land tenure.[13] In 1731 Henrietta Howard fortunately inherited property from her brother-in-law and became the Countess of Suffolk. In 1734, after the death of her estranged husband, she retired from court and remarried the next year. Pope commented, 'there is a greater Court now at Marble Hill than at Kensington and God knows

The survey of Marble Hill which shows it with a garden like the villas of the ancients with hippodrome, verdant arcade and winding walks.

where it will end'.[14] This is the most likely time for further work to have been undertaken in the garden. By then gardening ideas had changed and the second survey shows a layout very different from the first fanciful plan, with its Pope 'tramgams'; it was now more suited to her Palladian villa according to the ideas of classical villa gardens promulgated by Robert Castell's *Villas of the Ancients Illustrated*.

Castell's prestigious book, paid for by Lord Burlington, with conjectural plans based on the translations of Pliny's descriptions of his villa gardens at Tuscum and Laurentum, was published in 1728, the year that Chiswick villa was completed; it was dedicated to the earl, who was likened to Pliny and Varro as the leading authority on gardens. The same year Henrietta Howard's villa had been hailed by Robert Morris, a kinsman of Roger Morris the builder of Marble Hill, in his *Defence of Ancient Architecture* as an example of true taste. He was the chief exponent of Lord Burlington's Palladianism and on the title-page of his book he quoted Pope's lines from his *Essay on Criticism*, which had long been Lord Burlington's guide:

Learn hence for Ancient Rules a just Esteem
To Copy Nature is to copy Them. [15]

Richard Bradley in his *General Treatise of Husbandry and Gardening*, dedicated to Burlington in 1726, inferred that Chiswick was an example of antique gardening as well as architecture. ''Tis from such excellent Examples as Your Lordship has given us that we may hope to see both our Buildings and Gardens brought to the highest Pitch of Perfection'. In 1728 Castell clarified those true 'Rules of the Ancients' for whom 'Your Lordship has on all Occasions manifested the greatest Regard'. Henrietta Howard, imbued with Burlingtonian ideas and the possessor of the most exquisite Palladian villa in England, could not have failed to show interest in an illustrated exposition of ancient villa gardening, which far surpassed Pope's literary interpretation of Homer's garden of Alcinous in his essay in *The Guardian* later to appear in his translation of the *Odyssey*.

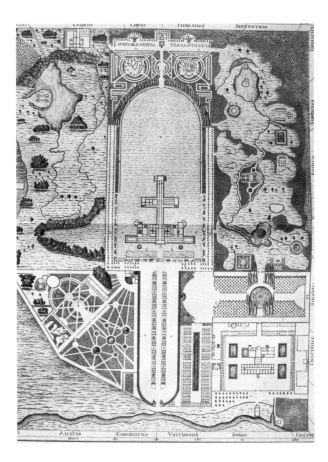

Robert Castell's *Villas of the Ancients Illustrated*, 1728, was dedicated to Lord Burlington the year Chiswick Villa was completed. This plate is a conjectural plan of Pliny's garden at Tuscum.

Right. Richard Wilson's painting of *The Thames near Marble Hill, Twickenham, circa* 1762, conveys a sense of the Arcadian scene so much enjoyed by Pope.

Joseph Spence affirmed that Lord Burlington liked to think of himself as having introduced the 'fine natural taste in gardening'[16] and Castell went out of his way to demonstrate that there was a classical precedent for the new irregular style of garden advocated by Shaftesbury, Pope, Addison, Switzer and Batty Langley in their writings. He added to the classical justification for irregularity the suggestion that the Chinese scorned regularity and planted in a natural way. Addison had written in 1711 that

the Chinese had a special word for such plantations laid out without 'Rule and Line'; according to Sir William Temple in his *Upon the Gardens of Epicurus* (1692) this was 'sharawadgi'. In 1725 Pope professed ignorance of the 'Sharawaggis of China' but presumed that, like other oriental imperial parks, they were 'very Great and very Wild'.[17] By 1728 Pliny's Roman layouts as delineated by Castell seemed much more achievable in the Home Counties.

The 'natural style' of the 'Villas of the Ancients' period was not 'beautiful nature' as Robinson thought it (see page 113) nor the picturesque relationship of building and garden that would be introduced by William Kent in the next decade; it was a mixture of regular and rural gardening adjacent to a strong central axis feature connecting the villa and the landscape. According to Castell, the ancients had apparently three distinct manners of gardening; to leave the ground in its rural state; plantations laid out 'by the Rule and Line' and 'Imitatio Ruris', which was a combination of both. Winding paths, so prominent in the Chiswick layout shown on the Rocque survey, were thought to be characteristic features of the classical gardens of Pliny and might also be construed as 'sharawadgi'. On the Marble Hill survey ordered quincunx groves contrast with 'imitatio ruris' and 'turning and winding paths' through woodland.

The main axial feature in the Marble Hill layout on the garden side of the villa, linking it to the river, is the elongated horse-shoe grass area, the traditional form for a Greek hippodrome adapted by the Romans to garden architecture and illustrated by Castell as being found in Pliny's gardens. The Rocque Chiswick survey of 1736 shows a similar shape in front of the villa; until 1733 there had remained a tightly planted grove 'not above 20ft distance from the new house' according to a visitor. Whereas at Chiswick the view from the villa was towards the hedged exedra, at Marble Hill the apsidal green shape was at the villa end and sloped down to allow an unobstructed view of the Thames. Henrietta Howard could not afford antique statues to grace exedra niches, as at Chiswick, but around the oval lawn in the immediate

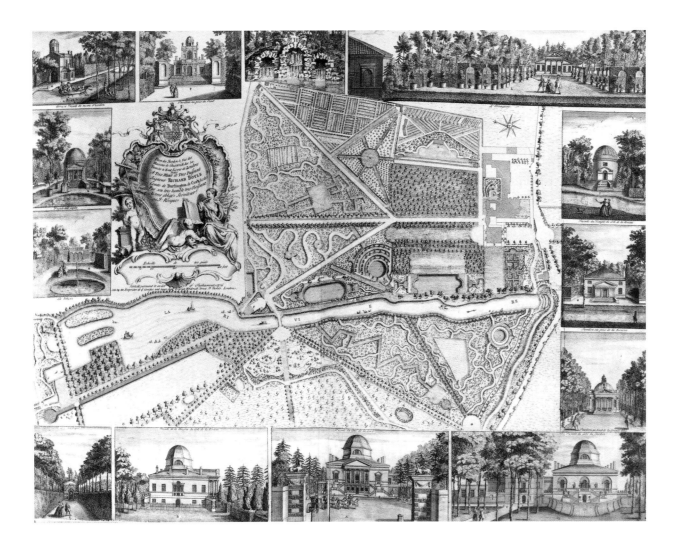

precincts of the villa there appears to be an evergreen palisade cut into an arcade comparable to that shown flanking Lord Burlington's orangery on the Rocque map. Bridgeman made such architectural use of natural material to give the effect of columns and arcades extensively at Stowe.

It is only to be expected that Bridgeman would be consulted by Henrietta Howard at Marble Hill again after the first 1724 'plann', for whatever reason, was discarded. Bridgeman was then working at Richmond Lodge, where Henrietta Howard was in attendance on the Princess Caroline, and in 1726 he gave advice to Pope about his

Twickenham garden. In March of that year Pope wrote to Bridgeman's patron, Edward Harley, 2nd Earl of Oxford, at Wimpole, where he was working, 'I have just turfed a little Bridgmannick Theatre myself. It was done by a detachment of His workmen from the Prince's, all at a stroke'.[18] In the mid 1730s Lady Suffolk was clearly still in touch with the royal gardener as she made the arrangements for his commission at Amesbury, the country seat of her great friend the Duchess of Queensberry. The layout shown on the Marble Hill survey has a much more professional 'Bridgmannick' look, than the previous 'plann' and, doubtless, as with the villa itself, reflected

John Rocque's engraved survey of Chiswick was published in 1736. It shows the would-be ancient garden layout and the villa as the grandest of the garden pavilions in the border vignettes.

its owner's interests, requirements and personality.

Now that Lady Suffolk spent more time at Marble Hill she would add more features for her own enjoyment; a room for her china and for the garden a grotto for which it was essential to have Pope's advice. There may have been an earlier simple grotto used as the icehouse which, as we know, Swift, 'robbed' when he was in England as he had the key to the wine cellar in her absence. The new grotto, now restored by English Heritage, was purely ornamental. In 1739 the countess wrote to Lord Pembroke, 'I am at this time over head and ears in shells'.[19] Pope was entering the second stage of his own geological 'grottofying' and could supply her not only with shells but with some of the Cornish material he was then receiving from William Borlase.

An interesting comparison with the Marble Hill layout is to be seen in the Rocque plan of Dalton Hall, made for Sir Charles Hotham, in 1737. The 5th Baronet was a great friend of Lord Burlington's and their wives were cousins; they often met at Londesborough, the Burlington Yorkshire estate a few miles away. Sir Charles was also well acquainted with Henrietta Howard. He first met her when the penniless Howards had resorted to the court at Hanover at the end of Queen Anne's reign and returned together in the train of George I. Charles

Hotham and Henrietta then both served in the court of the future of George II.

Charles Hotham clearly admired Henrietta's Marble Hill, as depicted in *Vitruvius Britannicus* in 1725, since Rocque shows a remarkably similar villa on the 1737 plan.[20] Sir Charles did not get the villa he coveted, however, as he died in 1738, but he had already laid out the garden in a style, which, like that of Marble Hill, would do credit to a villa of the ancients; it included the Pavilion, based on the gate of Burlington House, as seen on the Rocque plan.

However, as it happened, the real Marble Hill would eventually be inherited by a Hotham. The 8th Baronet married Henrietta Howard's niece, Dorothy Hobart, and it was their daughter Henrietta Hotham, born in 1752, who spent much time with her great aunt in her declining years. In 1765 she wrote to her parents that she had 'worked so hard in the Grotto and Rock that it is fear'd I shall damage my fingers'.[21] In 1767 Horace Walpole reported, 'I have been very unfortunate in the death of my Lady Suffolk, who was the only sensible friend I had at Strawberry'. She died in 1767 and the property went into trust and then to her nephew, the 2nd Earl of Buckinghamshire. Henrietta Hotham finally acquired Marble Hill in 1793.

1. BL Add.MS. 22625, f.123. Quoted in Peter Martin, *Pursuing Innocent Pleasures*, 1984, p.181.
2. *Correspondence*, 2:436. Pope and his friends seem to have camped out in the hall; Morris was still receiving payment for finishing the principal storey in 1729.
3. *Correspondence*, 2:240.
4. *Correspondence*, 2:256.
5. *Correspondence*, 2:264.
6. *Correspondence*, 2:261.
7. Martin, pp.46-47.
8. *Correspondence*, 3:191.
9. William Mason, *The English Garden*, Book 2, line 48.
10. The plate showing Langley's proposal for Johnston's garden in Twickenham was reversed and called anonymously 'a

beautiful garden in Twickenham'. It is clear that his proposed 'arti-natural' improvements were only conjectural.
11. BL Add MS 22626 f.9, quoted by Peter Martin.
12. *Correspondence*, 2:436.
13. David Jacques, 'Land Tenure at Marble Hill', unpublished report, 1995.
14. *Correspondence*, 3:478.
15. *Essay on Criticism*, ll.139-40
16. Spence, *Observations*, no.1121.
17. *Correspondence*, 2:314-15.
18. *Correspondence*, 2:372.
19. Wilton Mss.
20. For Dalton Hall, see David Neave, 'Lord Burlington's park and gardens at Londesborough', *Garden History*, vol.8, no.1 (1980)
21. A.M.W.Stirling, The Hothams, 1918, vol.2, p.95.

'CONSULT THE GENIUS OF THE PLACE IN ALL'

Pieter Andreas Rysbrack's painting of the view from across the new gardens towards the Bagnio at Chiswick shows the laying out of the winding paths. They were thought to be a characteristic feature of Pliny's gardens, which, in 1728, might also be construed as 'sharawadgi' or as an example of Langley's new arti-natural principles.

To build, to plant, whatever you intend,
To rear the Column, or the Arch to bend,
To swell the Terras, or to sink the Grot;
In all, let Nature never be forgot.
But treat the Goddess like a modest fair,
Nor over-dress, nor leave her wholly bare;
Let not each beauty ev'ry where be spy'd,
Where half the skill is decently to hide.
He gains all points, who pleasingly confounds,
Surprizes, varies, and conceals the Bounds.
Consult the Genius of the Place in all;
That tells the Waters or to rise, or fall,
Or helps th'ambitious Hill the heav'n to scale,
Or scoops in circling theatres the Vale,
Calls in the Country, catches op'ning glades,
Joins willing woods, and varies shades from shades,
Now breaks or now directs, th'intending Lines;
Paints as you plant, and, as you work, designs.
Still follow Sense, of ev'ry Art the Soul,
Parts answ'ring parts shall slide into a whole,
Spontaneous beauties all around advance,
Start ev'n from Difficulty, strike from Chance;
Nature shall join you, Time shall make it grow
A Work to wonder at – perhaps a STOW.

Alexander Pope, *Epistle IV, To Richard Boyle, Earl of Burlington,
Of the Use of Riches*, 1731, lines 47-70.

B

Y 1731 WHEN HE CAME TO WRITE THE FOURTH of his *Moral Essays* Alexander Pope was ready to convert his tentative gardening philosophy into guiding principles; significantly this essay was addressed to Burlington. The *Epistle to the Earl of Burlington* showed Pope's esteem for his patron's lead in promoting taste through 'good sense'. He said that he had for some time wished to 'leave some testimony for your Lordship among my writing' and the occasion was, as the sub-title to the *Epistle* stated, the earl's publication in 1730 of Palladio's *Designs of the Baths, Arches, Theatres etc of Ancient Rome*:

> *You show us, Rome was glorious, not profuse,*
> *And pompous buildings once were things of use.*

Having praised the earl as an arbiter of architectural taste, Pope then turned to his own new thoughts on landscape gardening. The *Epistle* was Pope's first public utterance on gardening since his essay in *The Guardian* in 1713, nearly twenty years before. His new thoughts were much more structured and instantly acclaimed; the *Guardian* essay had been anonymous and was often attributed to the editor, Richard Steele. By 1731 Pope's concise, epigrammatical remarks in his various works had taken on the force of proverbs: 'Fools rush in where angels fear to tread'; 'A little learning is a dangerous thing'. Now his landscaping maxims, pronounced with the same Horatian skill, became rallying cries for those laying out country estates: 'Let not each beauty ev'ry where be spy'd'; 'Consult the Genius of the Place in all'.

The *Epistle* was written to his patron while Pope was very much under the influence of Bolingbroke and his stand on corruption and the misuse of wealth. It is a tribute to Lord Burlington's good sense, taste, and right 'use of riches' in architecture and gardening at Chiswick, comparing it with the 'vanity of expense' of the so-called 'Timon's villa' with its owner's 'false Taste of Magnificence'.[1] We learn from John Macky that as early as 1718 the young earl already 'hath a good Taste' in

painting and gardening, and, as we know, music. Pope had found his gardens round the old Chiswick House 'delightfull' and his music 'ravishing' when he was living nearby in 1716.[2]

Lord Burlington had set out to promote Shaftesbury's Whig 'national taste' in gardening even before he extended it to architecture after his return from his Grand Tour. Shaftesbury, who rejected the inflexibility of the Cartesian system of philosophy, also decried the baroque 'formal Mockery of princely Gardens', such as those of Versailles, which were conceived as a finished product and were manifestations of the same rigid system. He called for greater respect for the 'genuine order' of nature. Pope's doctrine – 'In all, let Nature never be forgot' – would likewise condemn a formal garden planned on a drawing-board without regard to the character of the site.

In his *Epistle to the Earl of Burlington* Pope called for a more flexible attitude, which 'as you work, designs'. His own small Twickenham garden was constantly changing and his 'visionary beauties' took time to grow. Le Nôtre had sent a design for royal Greenwich without ever setting foot in England and Daniel Marot had designed the parterres at Hampton Court for William III as the overall decorative designer of the palace.[3] Pope's owner of taste in the Burlington mould, who would himself direct his landscape improvements, would prefer 'spontaneous beauties' and, as stated in the prefatorial Argument, would seek to adapt all 'to the Genius and Use of the Place, and the Beauties not forced into it, but resulting from it'.

Stephen Switzer, who in 1715 in his first gardening treatise had already adapted Pope's general classical precepts in the *Essay on Criticism* for his own ends (see page 33), was quick to echo the new specific guidelines in a later post-*Epistle* edition of *Ichnographia Rustica*. With renewed authority he advised every garden designer to 'submit to Nature, and not Nature to his Design' by

Overleaf. Part of the patte d'oie at Chiswick painted by Pieter Andreas Rysbrack. The alleys are terminated by Burlington's buildings and are lined by French clipped hedges with, as in Pliny, the trunks of trees wreathed in ivy to give 'borrowed verdure'.

'adapting the whole to the Nature and Uses of the Place, for which your Design is formed'.[4]

While promoting a 'national' and more 'natural taste' in gardening Burlington would still be influenced by French techniques and conjectural classical gardens. In the year 1728, the year of Castell's *Villas of the Ancients*, Lord Burlington also subscribed to the second enlarged edition of John James's *The Theory and Practice of Gardening*, a translation of A.J. Dezallier d'Argenville's book, which codified the French grand style of Le Nôtre.

The first stage of Burlington's gardening had been to provide settings for his garden buildings in the grounds of the old Chiswick House, which John Macky, in his *A Journey through England* in 1724 said were the 'effect of his Lordship's own genius, and singular fine taste':

Every walk terminates with some little Building, one with a Heathen Temple, for instance the Pantheon, another a little villa, where my Lord often dines instead of his House, … another walk terminates with a Portico, in imitation of Covent Garden Church.[5]

The general intention of the early layout at Chiswick can be seen in the Rocque map of 1736, commissioned by Burlington (see page 84). Although the new Palladian villa had been built by then the plan shows how the temples and pavilions dominate the layout in which the villa itself had come to be seen as the largest and most elegant of the garden buildings.

The Rysbrack paintings of about 1728 show the first stage of Burlington's garden completed before William Kent appeared on the scene; the *patte d'oie* with its three vistas each terminating in a building, the *allées* being lined with high green clipped hedges in the French fashion to heighten the effect; the Ionic temple and obelisk in a circular pond; the canal with the Bagnio, Lord Burlington's first essay in architecture. *The Pond and the Temple* (see page 34) shows sculpturally moulded banks and tree boles; at the head of the formally shaped pond clipped hedges form an exedra contrasting with naturally growing trees behind. Rigaud also drew this view showing Pope in the foreground (page 27).[6] When the new

villa was nearing completion Burlington acquired the land on the other side of the Bollar Brook, which Rysbrack shows being laid out with serpentine walks, bordered with clipped hedges (page 87).

Variety, concealment and surprise, as with Pope's garden at Twickenham, were the hallmarks of Chiswick. In Pope's words in the *Epistle*:

Let not each beauty ev'ry where be spyed,
Where half the skill is decently to hide.

Le Nôtre created great level spaces with parterres round the house with a main elongated vista on its axis and trees pushed well back to display the great house to advantage. Dr Bradley writing in 1725 condemned such designs where 'we see all at once and lose the Pleasure of Expectation' and pointed to the gardens of 'the Earl of Burlington's at Chiswick, where the Contrivance and Disposition of the Several Parts, sufficiently declare the grand Taste of the Master'.[7]

We must turn to Joseph Spence, Pope's Boswell, for an exposition of those principles, finally set out in the *Epistle to the Earl of Burlington*, which would guide future garden design in England. By then Spence had acquired a rectory at Birchanger in Essex and was able to indulge his passion for gardening himself inspired by his mentor. He planned to have statues of Homer, Virgil, Milton and Pope in his garden. Spence and Pope also discussed landscaping ideas with their good friend Philip Southcote, and these were incorporated into Spence's *Observations*. Southcote, the nephew of Thomas Southcote, who had been of service to the young Pope at the outset of his crippling disease, laid out Woburn Farm near Chertsey in 1735 as a ferme ornée.[8]

Pope, who had praised the 'untrimmed farm' and 'the useful Part of Horticulture' in his early essay in *The Guardian*, was greatly in favour of the ornamental farm with its Horatian purposes of pleasure and profit which developed in the Thames valley; in addition to Bolingbroke's Dawley Farm and Bathurst's Riskins he admired Lord Halifax's 'delightful Abbs Court' in Molesey. Sheep were kept on lawns round the houses and the insides of the quarters of the wildernesses were planted with crops for feeding cattle. According to Spence, Southcote was the first to call such grounds a 'ferme ornée' and to introduce natural planting in them. At Woburn Farm he planted a perimeter flowery shrubbery walk around the grazing grounds which would have much influence on later garden design.[9]

Spence told a friend that Pope's own ideas were contained in the two lines of the *Epistle*:

He gains all Ends, who pleasingly confounds,
Surprises, varies and conceals the bounds.

He elaborated on Pope's instructions: 'to vary the scenes, lights and shades, colours of leaves etc; to hide what is disagreeable near you and take in what is agreeable, to extend the appearance of your ground, call in the country' and only to design on the spot having consulted every aspect of the Genius of the Place.[10]

A note is added in Spence's *Observations* that in this new garden philosophy there is 'nothing of this in the rules, or facts, delivered down to us from the ancients'; by 1731 it had become clear that the so-called natural taste of the ancients, so beloved of Burlington, was no longer viable. Pope, in fact, does not mention the authority of the ancients in the *Epistle* and Burlington could understandably be rather peeved that the poem, in spite of its dedication to his good taste, goes out of its way to commend Stowe. Walpole would later make the point that Alcinous's garden had little to commend it once 'divested of harmonious Greek and bewitching poetry' and so far as villas of the ancients were concerned 'all the ingredients of Pliny's corresponded with those laid out by London and Wise on Dutch principles'.[11] Indeed a Frenchman translated Pliny's Letters in a way which showed that classical antiquity was the precedent for Le Nôtre's garden design.[12]

The extent to which Pope had assisted Robert Castell with his translations or approved of the type of Pliny garden design he advocated is unclear. There was, however, a different type of classical inspiration for English gardening where Pope's poetic influence was undoubtedly paramount; this was the idea of the 'locus amoenus', the background of pastoral poetry, the Elysian fields where the blessed enjoyed eternal bliss; it had nothing to do with the villa gardens where Pliny entertained his fellow mortal Romans in AD100. William Mason, writing in the

Right. A Claudian Elysian landscape at Stowe. The 'locus amoenus' of pastoral poetry 'imaged' by Pope into real landscape scenes had little to do with ancient villa gardening; it had a common source with Claude's paintings of the golden age of classical mythology.

Luke Sullivan's drawing of the ferme ornée at Woburn Farm. Pope was a friend of Southcote and admired this ornamental farm at Weybridge.

1770s when natural landscaping was well established, was able to put the role of the ancients in perspective:

> *Meanwhile, of old and classic aid*
> *Tho' fruitless be the search, your eyes entranc'd*
> *Shall catch those glowing scenes, that taught a Claude*
> *To grace his canvas with Hesperian hues.*[13]

The poetic mythology that Claude Lorrain had captured in the 'glowing scenes' of his paintings set in the Roman Campagna and its association with temples dedicated to gods, heroes and virtues was no more apparent than at Stowe. Pope's friend and fellow poet James Thomson described in 1744, in his extended 'Autumn', how Lord Cobham's Buckinghamshire garden evoked a classical landscape of the golden age for him:

> *While there…th'inchanted Round I walk.*
> *The regulated Wild, gay Fancy then*
> *Will tread in Thought the Groves of Attic lands.*[14]

Pope's poetic influence was duly acknowledged when he was enshrined in the Temple of the British Worthies at Stowe and his 'Consult the Genius of the Place' lines ending with 'A Work to wonder at – perhaps a STOW' were set out on the tablet on the north side of the Cobham monument erected in 1747; on the south side was an extract from another *Moral Essay*, Pope's *Epistle to Sir Richard Temple, Lord Cobham*, praising his 'ruling passion' of patriotism. Lord Cobham had recently given up his career as a statesman to join the 'Patriot' opposition which accused Sir Robert Walpole of abandoning Whig principles of liberty. An inscription pointed out that Cobham's dual claim to fame, celebrated by Pope, lay in that he had 'served his country well in the Cabinet and in the field, and adorned it with a more elegant concept of gardening first revealed in these grounds'.

In 1731 Pope's friend, Cobham's nephew, Gilbert West, who, as we have seen, later took ideas for the Stowe grotto from Twickenham, wrote a long poem on the gardens; it was dedicated to Pope and had been sent to him for approval. West saw Stowe as 'the British Iliad' where poetic imaging and landscape planting went hand in hand:

> To Thee, great Master of the vocal String,
> O Pope. Of Stowe's Elyzian Scenes I sing:
> That Stowe, which better far thy Muse divine
> Command to live in one distinguish'd Line.
> The same presiding Muse alike inspires
> The Planter's Spirit and the Poet's Fires…,
> All great, all perfect Works from genius flow,
> The British Iliad hence, and hence the Groves of Stowe.[15]

Such was the force of Pope's praise that the 'one distinguished line' where he referred to 'A Work to wonder at – perhaps a STOW' helped to establish Stowe's international reputation. West was a good classical scholar and he and Pope undoubtedly co-operated on the classical iconography, set out in West's 'poetick plan' of Stowe; the route given was followed by all subsequent guidebooks and tourists. His descriptions of the contrast between clipped hedges and 'native wilder beauties', 'living Colonnades', 'verdant arches', a profusion of temples, 'windings of the Mazy Wood' seem to suggest Chiswick on a larger scale. Bridgeman, who was employed at Stowe soon after 1719, in collaboration with Vanbrugh, had undoubtedly been much involved in the design.

In 1733 Bridgeman invited Rigaud from France to make a series of views which complement West's poetic guide and show the Stowe that Pope so much admired.[16] Rigaud made a similar record of Chiswick at this time, and it is possible that Bridgeman may also have been consulted at an early stage of the laying out of the gardens by Lord Burlington. The Chiswick drawings were never engraved but the perspective views of Stowe, dedicated to Lord Cobham, were published by Bridgeman's widow in 1739 as a memorial to his co-operation with a gardening lord. Bridgeman had died the previous year and the Stowe engravings are an important record of garden design in the 1720s and 30s.

Pope always returned to Stowe with 'fresh satisfaction' and just before he wrote the *Epistle* he had taken another 'summer ramble' to Stowe. 'If anything under Paradise could set me beyond all Earthly Cogitations, Stowe might do it. It is much more beautyful this year – much enlarged and with variety'.[17] The Home Park had been taken into the gardens nearly doubling their size and Bridgeman had added the Eleven-Acre lake. The lines in the *Epistle*: 'The vast Parterres a thousand hands shall make/Lo! Bridgman comes and floats them with a lake', apparently offended him but Pope denied it was 'a fling at honest Bridgman'. However, in the next edition of the *Epistle* Pope changed 'Bridgman' to Cobham, who was undoubtedly in overall charge of the improvements, and tried to put the record straight. 'Is it not his business to please gentlemen? to execute Gentlemen's will and Pleasure, not his own?' he said in his explanatory 'Master Key to Popery'.[18]

Switzer took the opportunity to criticise his professional rival in 1742, after Bridgeman's death, for 'aiming at an incomprehensible Vastness' and the plan of his lakes 'which he generally designed so large, as to make the whole Country look like an Ocean'.[19] He was here quoting from Pope's ridicule of the layout of 'Timon's Villa' in the *Epistle*.

Below.
William Hogarth's
frontispiece to
A Miscellany on Taste
by Mr Pope etc. The
satire was published
soon after the
publication of Pope's
Epistle to the Earl of
Burlington.

Left. An engraving of the view of the Queen's Theatre from the Rotonda at Stowe. It shows a layout of the early Bridgeman stage with a crude 'calling in' of the country.

Greatness, with Timon, dwells in such a draught
As brings all Brobdignag before your thought
To compass this, his building is a Town
His pond an Ocean, his parterre a Down.

Pope's critics took this not as a jibe at Bridgeman but at the Duke of Chandos and his ostentatious seat at Cannons in Middlesex. Pope denied this, saying that Timon was 'a character applied to twenty' and intended only to demonstrate 'a false taste of Magnificence'. Timon's style of gardening was, however, exactly what the new 'good taste' of Burlington and Cobham had rejected. Everything was laid out for show to complement the opulent house and as Macky said, 'You see the whole at once, be in what part of the garden or parterre you will';[20] there was nothing 'Soft and Agreeable' in the 'natural taste' as there was at Chiswick and Stowe.

No pleasing Intricacies intervene,
No artful Wilderness to perplex the Scene;
Grove nods at Grove, each Ally has a brother.[21]

Pope continued to be pilloried for what was seen to be a castigation of the Duke of Chandos and in a letter attached to Burlington's copy of the third edition of the *Epistle* he announced that in future he would probably use 'real names and not fictitious ones' to 'avoid misconstructions'. The next *Epistle* was to Lord Bathurst in 1732 and contains a tribute to a real person, John Kyrle, the 'Man of Ross', praising his right use of riches. Kyrle was not just a good gentleman farmer, like Pope's friend Bethel, but a local benefactor and provider of a public park for the citizens of Ross with a viewpoint down to the river Wye.[22]

William Hogarth, the year following Pope's *Epistle to the Earl of Burlington*, kept up the Chandos 'false taste' attribution when he caricatured Taste as set out by Pope; the poet is seen 'bespattering' with whitewash the Duke of Chandos and all and sundry beneath, while the architect earl, with his newly acquired garter, ascends the ladder of Taste. At the very top of the Burlington House gate is William Kent. The painter, seen here with his palette, is poised to take off into a new career of architecture and landscape gardening which would transform eighteenth-century taste.

1. *Moral Essays: Epistle IV to Richard Boyle, Earl of Burlington*, introductory Argument to verse 97.
2. *Correspondence*, 1:338.
3. See Mavis Batey and David Lambert, *The English Garden Tour*, 1990. Greenwich, p.67. See also Mavis Batey and Jan Woudstra, *The Story of the Privy Garden at Hampton Court*, 1996.
4. Stephen Switzer, from 'A Prooemial Essay' to Volume 1, 1742; set out in *The Genius of the Place*, p.154.
5. John Macky, 1724, vol.1, p.87.
6. John Harris drew attention to this in *The Palladian Revival, Lord Burlington, His Villa and Garden at Chiswick*, 1994, p.102.
7. Richard Bradley, *Survey of the ancient husbandry and gardening*, p.361. He dedicated his next book, *General Treatise of Husbandry and Gardening*, 1726, to Burlington.
8. See R.W.King, 'Philip Southcote and Woburn Farm', *Garden History*, vol.2, no.3 (1974), pp.27-60.
9. Ibid.
10. Letter to the Rev. Mr. Wheeler (on gardening), 1751. Reprinted in *The Genius of the Place*, p.268.
11. *Modern Gardening*, p.239.
12. See H.Tanzer, *The Villas of Pliny the Younger*, 1924.
13. William Mason, *The English Garden*, Book I, ll.63-66.
14. James Thomson, *The Seasons*, 'Autumn' (1744), ll.1054-57.
15. Gilbert West, *Stowe, the Gardens of the Right Honorable Richard Lord Viscount Cobham* (1732). Reprinted in full in *Descriptions of Lord Cobham's Gardens at Stowe 1700-1759*, ed. G.B.Clarke, 1990.
16. See Peter Willis, 'Jacques Rigaud's Drawings of Stowe in the Metropolitan Museum of Art', *18th Century Studies*, vol. VI, no.1, Jan.1972, pp.85-98.
17. *Correspondence*, 3:217.
18. This was never published in his lifetime, and was first noted in Lady Burlington's hand and printed by John Butt, 'A Master Key to Popery' in *Pope and his Contemporaries. Essays presented to George Sherburn*, ed. J.L.Clifford, 1949, pp.41-57. See also M.Brownell, *Alexander Pope and the Arts of Georgian England*, 1978, p.168.
19. See note 4.
20. John Macky, 1722, 9-10.
21. *Epistle to the Earl of Burlington*, ll.115-17.
22. See Howard Erskine-Hill, *The social Milieu of Alexander Pope*, 1975, pp.16-41, for an account of Pope's connection with the Man of Ross.

'PAINTS AS YOU PLANT AND AS YOU WORK DESIGNS'

The Temple of Venus at Stowe. This was probably Kent's first
garden building (*circa* 1730) and would lead him on to
Pope-inspired landscape gardening.

AT THAT MOMENT appeared Kent, painter enough to taste the charms of landscape, bold and opinionative enough to dare and to dictate, and born with a genius to strike out a great system from the twilight of imperfect essays. He leaped the fence, and saw that all nature was a garden. He felt the delicious contrast of hill and valley changing imperceptibly into each other, tasted the beauty of the gentle swell, or concave scoop, and remarked how loose groves crowned an easy eminence with happy ornament, and while they called in the distant view between their graceful stems, removed and extended the perspective by delusive comparison.

Thus the pencil of his imagination bestowed all the arts of landscape on the scenes he handled. The great principles on which he worked were perspective, and light and shade. Groupes of trees broke too uniform or too extensive a lawn, evergreens and woods were opposed to the glare of the champain, and where the view was less fortunate, or so much exposed as to be beheld at once, he blotted out some parts by thick shades, to divide it into variety, or to make the richest scene more enchanting by reserving it to a farther advance of the spectator's step. Thus selecting favourite objects, and veiling deformities by screens of plantation; sometimes allowing the rudest waste to add its foil to the richest theatre, he realised the composition of the greatest masters in painting. Where objects were wanting to animate his horizon, his taste as an architect could bestow immediate termination. His buildings, his seats, his temples, were more the works of his pencil than of his compasses. We owe the restoration of Greece and the diffusion of architecture to his skill in landscape.

Horace Walpole, *On Modern Gardening*, 1782, from *Anecdotes of Painting*, ed. Dallaway, 1827, pages 264-65.

WILLIAM KENT UNDOUBTEDLY OWED HIS successful career to his patron Lord Burlington; it was indeed fortunate that he met the earl in Rome and came back with him to be installed as a lifelong companion at Burlington House. Although Kent was originally employed as a painter he soon adopted the role of versatile artist through Burlington's introductions. One thing led to another, interior decoration, furniture, silverware, a royal barge, temples and hermitages; as George Vertue noted, 'Mr Kent at Court and amongst people of quality, call'd on for drafts and on all occasions'.[1] Lady Burlington, Pope's 'Pallas', enjoyed a very good humoured relationship with Kent; he taught her to sketch and, as lady-in-waiting to Queen Caroline, she was in a good position to advance his interests with royal commissions.[2]

When he turned to landscape gardening in the early 1730s Kent's greatest debt was to Alexander Pope from whom he had learned an appreciation of poetic landscape and with whom he had discussed the principles of landscaping that had been set out in the poet's *Epistle to the Earl of Burlington*. Kent also profited from Pope's ideas on painterly perspective planting which the poet used with such success in his own garden. William Shenstone, the poet-gardener, was the first, in 1764, in his *Unconnected Thoughts on Gardening*, to call the new landscaping art that Kent introduced 'picturesque gardening'.

Pope was one of the first to use the expression 'picturesque' in English when he spoke of the 'imaging and picturesque parts' of Homer[3] and the word was clearly synonymous with 'imaging' or scenes 'painted to the mind' while reading epic or pastoral poetry. William Gilpin, the pioneer of the later Picturesque movement, was much influenced by Pope as a poet and moralist and in matters of taste. His early works were prefaced by quotations from 'Windsor Forest'. When Gilpin was a schoolmaster at Cheam in the 1750s he encouraged his pupils to cultivate a 'picture-making faculty' when reading descriptive passages in the classics as Pope had done and listed for them what he found 'picturesque' in the *Aeneid*: a hero resting after battle, a sea nymph pushing a ship or a wolf running away in fear.[4] These were heroic attitudes suitable for a history painting and consistent with Pope's use of the word as verbal painting.

Gilpin would later change the concept of the Picturesque when he suggested that a 'picture imagination' might also be an agreeable accompaniment to travel and enable the tourist to seek out scenery a painter would wish to paint. This would be three decades after the deaths of Pope and Kent, who were never involved with this type of picturesque activity. Like the Cheam schoolboys, Kent's first picturesque excursion was not painting natural scenery but seeking out descriptive passages of poetry to illustrate. In 1720 he was invited to illustrate the *Poems on Several Occasions* by his friend John Gay who was a fellow resident at Burlington House and, in 1727, his *Fables*; one of the plates for the latter shows a garden with a green arcade, statues and a building clearly meant to be his patron's Bagnio at Chiswick (see over). In 1725 Kent illustrated Pope's *Odyssey* and included a version of Calypso's grotto (see page 63).

Illustrations for the collected volumes of Thomson's *The Seasons* in 1730 gave Kent more scope for his imagination. Thomson had arrived in London in 1725 and soon became a member of the Burlington set. He owned his indebtedness as a poet to Pope and in 'Winter', in 1726, he spoke of their friendship. Pope wrote the Prologue to Thomson's tragedy *Sophonisba* in 1729. Thomson delighted in taking long walks and viewing the metropolis from the surrounding hills, particularly enjoying the view from Richmond Hill. 'Heavens! What a goodly prospect spreads around'.[5] Pope's description of the countryside in his pastoral poetry paved the way for a more romantic appreciation of nature, but Thomson struck a new naturalistic note with immediate effect. In

Dr Johnson's words: 'The reader of the "Seasons" wonders that he never saw before what Thomson shews him, and that he never yet has felt what Thomson impresses'.

Kent's frontispiece for 'Spring' combined pastoral imagery with Thomson's eulogy of extended landscape in an Arcadian scene where swains allow their eyes to 'roam excursive' with arms outstretched towards a classical villa river landscape. 'Spring' shows a villa with portico and undercroft grotto, a grander Twickenham, and 'Autumn' has a domed villa with Diocletian window and more than a hint of Chiswick. Imbued with these poetic ideas, Kent was able to transform the time-honoured image of the 'locus amoenus' of pastoral poetry, impressed on him by Pope, with Thomson's new cult of perceiving beauty in prospect into picturesque garden scenes; in the words of Isaac Ware, a Burlington associate, 'what had so long ravished in the idea, now appeared in reality'.

Kent and Pope, who called poetry 'a speaking Picture', both upheld the Horatian theme of *Ut pictura poesis* (as with the painter's work, so with the poet's). Kent was able to enhance his ideas of poetic landscape by studying Claude Lorrain's drawings when the Duke of Devonshire acquired his *Liber Veritatis* for the library of his Piccadilly house in 1727.[6] In Burlington's own collection he had access to Inigo Jones's drawings of masque

Above left. William Kent's illustration of Gay's fable '*The Butterfly and the Snail*', 1727, is given a Chiswick setting showing Burlington's architectural use of natural materials.

Above. Kent's frontispiece for Thomson's 'Spring' in *The Seasons.*

The Hermitage at Stowe. Here and at Richmond the hermitages were real versions of Kent's illustration of the deceitful Archimago's cell in Book One of *The Faerie Queene.*

settings, which added the theatrical dimension to his ideas for picturesque scenes in gardens. He probably also studied Matteo Ripa's album of drawings of Jehol.[7]

Kent considered Spenser's *The Faerie Queene* to be the best work for picturesque image-making and produced thirty two illustrations for an edition which was not finally published until after his death in 1748. It was almost certainly Pope who introduced Kent to the charms of Spenserian fancy. Spence recorded Pope's own love of Spenser; he read *The Faerie Queene* to his elderly mother who likened it to a 'gallery of pictures'.[8] Spenser blended classic epic with chivalric romance and so allowed native legends, with knights errant rather than Greek heroes, to flourish in a way which appealed to

Kent. In his *Letters on Chivalry and Romance* Bishop Hurd, also a Spenser admirer, regretted that the Enlightenment, although disposing of omens and prodigies, had lost a 'world of fine fabling'.[9] He related Kent's method of gardening to Spenser's gothic poetry and William Mason reported that Kent 'frequently declared he caught his taste in Gardening from reading the picturesque descriptions of Spenser'.[10] There are certainly echoes of Kent's gardening taste in his illustrations to *The Faerie Queene*, particularly in Phaedria's Island with its picturesque landscape and recognisable Kentian features.

Kent's garden buildings led on to his career as a landscape gardener and, as with Lord Burlington, they would also pave the way to his becoming an architect. An early involvement was with Pope's shell temple, which Kent illustrated prominently in his capriccio of the poet's garden as a classical scene with gods happily settled at the end of a rainbow at Twickenham complete with sacrificial altar, antique tripod and bust of Homer; at the other end of the picture the artist is seen with his arm round the poet and Bounce very much in evidence (see page 65). The scene is reminiscent of Pope's 'Summer' pastoral: 'Descending Gods have found Elysium here'. A whimsical temple is known to have been in existence in 1725 and Kent may well have been involved even then; he certainly seems to have had a hand in the rebuilding when it fell down in 1735 and also designed similar ones at Stowe outside the grotto (see page 62). Kent is known to have helped his friend with a portico for the villa in 1732 as Pope wrote to Burlington, who was still paying for the building materials, to seek his approval of the plan. Kent was now Kent the architect in the earl's eyes and he wrote, a trifle condescendingly, that he had 'considered your front and am of opinion that my friend Kent has done all that can be, considering the place'.[11]

Stowe was probably Kent's first essay in 'practical poetry',[12] the visual embodiment of poetic ideas, in the form of garden buildings in a *Faerie Queene* setting. He had built the Temple of Venus (see page 97) by the time Cobham's nephew, Gilbert West, a fellow Spenser addict, wrote his poem on Stowe, dedicated to Pope, in 1732; about the same time the temple was illustrated by Isaac Ware in his *Designs of Inigo Jones and Others*.

Fair on the Brow, a spacious Building stands,
Th' applauded Work of Kent's judicious Hands.[13]

Murals on the temple by Sleter depict the before and after story of Malbecco and the unfaithful Hellenore. West suggests that the cave where Malbecco saw the 'Satyrs and Fauns their wanton Frolicks play' was Kent's nearby hermitage, which he later reproduced in his *Faerie Queene* illustrations.[14]

An almost identical hermitage was built for Richmond gardens at about the same time. There was no nonsense about Venus and suggestive male murals of

'wanton frolicks' in Queen Caroline's hermitage; it was an intellectual scene dedicated to natural scientists and philosophers with busts of Newton, Locke, Samuel Clarke and Wollaston to prove it; nevertheless in Kent's capriccio of the Richmond Arcadia he includes a satyr paying decorous homage to a royal shepherdess. Although the hermitage had a rustic appearance it was furnished inside with stylish bookcases and couches. A few years later Kent built Merlin's Cave for Queen Caroline, who collected romance writings and saw

Above. William Kent's drawing of the Hermitage at Richmond in a Bridgeman setting. 'Arcadia' is written over the door.

Left. Two of Kent's illustrations for Spenser's *The Faerie Queene.*
Top. Phaedria's Island in Book Two features Kentian landscape buildings.
Below. Despair is encountered by the Red Cross Knight in a cavern surrounded by dead trees and skeletons.

Overleaf. The exedra at Chiswick as executed by Kent according to Burlington's wishes.

herself not only as the patron of natural gardening, 'helping nature and not losing it in art' as she put it, but also, like Spenser, a champion of revived national identity.[15] Merlin's Cave was a gothic venture with three thatched bee-hive shaped domes; inside were waxwork tableaux of Tudor monarchs recalling Merlin's prophecy that the ancient kings of Britain would return to power. Stephen Duck, the 'thresher-poet', was appointed as the librarian.

At Richmond the royal gardener, Bridgeman, was still developing the garden and Kent's gothic buildings were anchored with terraces and earthworks to his overall design. The royal gardening commission at Kensington gave Kent a freer hand. Bridgeman had completed the work there by 1731, and when Kent came to design the Queen's Temple overlooking the new Serpentine river in 1735 he was able to cut swathes into the existing formal planting to create small, enticingly glimpsed picturesque scenes; the temple was sited on an open sloping lawn and was reflected in the water.

Caroline died in 1737 but there may have been an intention to create a cave in a Kentian gothic setting, more realistic than the Bridgeman setting for his Merlin's Cave at Richmond. This would account for Walpole's claim that at Kensington Kent 'planted dead trees, to give a greater air of truth to the scene';[16] all reminiscent of his illustration for the *Faerie Queene* episode where the Knight of the Red Cross, the hero of the book of Holinesse, encountered and conquered Despair in a cavern surrounded by dead trees.

> *And all about old stockes and stubs of trees,*
> *Whereon nor fruit, nor leafe was ever seene.*

Walpole said that Kent was 'soon laughed out of this excess' helped perhaps by Pope's lines on an appropriate abode for a country mouse; 'As sweet a Cave as one shall see! A most romantic hollow Tree! A pretty kind of savage Scene'.[17]

Pope often teased Kent about being a 'wild goth'. Writing, in 1734, to Burlington from Tottenham Park, which the earl had designed for his brother-in-law, Pope jokingly said, obviously with every intention of it being passed on to Kent, 'I am told this man hath suggested an odd thing, which thro his Violence of Temper and Ungovernable Spirit of Dominion (natural to all Goths) he will infallibly erect; unless I lay a Temple in his way, which he will probably not venture to pull down'.[18] This was typical Pope banter with Kent, however, and in a later letter to the earl he would speak of 'the affection I bear him, and the respect I pay to his genius'.[19]

Kent's first commission to design a new garden, rather than garden buildings, was for the Prince of Wales's Carlton House in the Mall in 1732. Pope, Lyttelton, Bolingbroke and Burlington had high hopes, culturally and politically, for Prince Frederick who had broken with his royal parents, and, as they had done at Richmond in a similar situation, wanted a court of his own. Kent was on hand in his new role as versatile artist at the prince's service. In 1731 he began to build the Palladian White House at Kew and for a masquerade designed a shepherd's costume for the prince and fantastic outfits for accompanying huntsmen. The following year he designed Frederick's elaborately carved and gilded state barge.[20] Carlton House had been owned by Lord Burlington but in 1732 it was transformed by William Kent for the Prince of Wales. In the garden the octagon pavilion was Burlingtonian but Walpole maintained that the design of the garden itself was 'evidently borrowed from the poet's at Twickenham'.[21]

Sir Thomas Robinson, an architect friend of Burlington, catches the moment when Kent's new ideas were beginning to change landscape taste; writing in 1734 he said:

There is a new taste in gardening just arisen, which has been practised with so great success at the Prince's garden in town, that a general alteration of some of the most considerable gardens in the kingdom is begun, after Mr Kent's notion of gardening, viz to lay them out without level or line…the celebrated gardens of Claremont, Chiswick and Stowe are now full of labourers, to modernise the expensive works finished in them, even since every one's memory.[22]

At Claremont some of the 'expensive works' for the Duke of Newcastle, such as Vanburgh's existing belvedere and Bridgeman's amphitheatre were retained, but Kent's labourers removed the bastion feature Bridgeman had

Right. **The Temple of the British Worthies at Stowe (the building originally intended for Burlington's exedra). Pope is enshrined as one of the Worthies.**

built and replaced it by a ha-ha and the lines of the avenues were broken. An irregular lake with an island and temple was created out of a formal pond and a favourite Kentian triple-arched grotto cascade built over the spring that fed the lake. In the early 1730s Claremont was, as Robinson observed, an early example of the new Kent 'notion of gardening' laid out in a pictorial manner.[23]

However 'bold and opinionative enough to dare and dictate'[24] Kent might be in suggesting improvements elsewhere, at Chiswick he would still be subject to ideas of 'his Lordship's happy Invention'. The gardens up to the 1730s were laid out according to Burlington's idea, although it is possible that he had the benefit of Bridgeman's assistance.[25] In 1733 the earl went into opposition and resigned all his offices. He symbolically cut off his association with the capital by making Chiswick his main residence and building a link communication between the old house and the villa. He removed his best pictures from Burlington House to Chiswick, and set about making further improvements to his gardens.

Kent was now able to cooperate in the earl's new gardening schemes. Spence gave a precise date of October 1733[26] for Kent's involvement at Chiswick and insisted that he was 'the sole beginner of the national taste', which Burlington had long wished to establish. Kent was not, however, allowed to extend his new 'without level or line' ideas to Burlington's own architectural part of the garden. The tight quincunx grove which came within feet of the north side of the villa was removed in 1733, but Kent's first design of a free standing building in a natural setting, with open views through to Burlington's Ionic temple, was rejected; it would later appear as the Temple of the British Worthies in Stowe's Elysian Fields. Burlington favoured instead a hippodrome from Castell's villas of the ancients and as an exedra statues of Caesar, Pompey and Cicero in evergreen niches, which Defoe said were from Hadrian's Villa; this remained screened from the earlier adjacent grass amphitheatre with its Ionic temple, which the earl had modelled on the Pantheon in Rome.

Kent was, however, seemingly given a freer hand on the west side of the villa to create a sloping lawn and to naturalise the lake and architectural cascade. Kent's rockwork rustic cascade seen on the Rocque map of 1736 (see page 84), now restored by English Heritage, was probably inspired by similar features, such as the rustic fountain at the Villa Aldobrandini, which he had seen in gardens during his ten year stay in Italy.[27] Kent clearly made frequent reference to his Italian experiences as he was affectionately called the Signor by the Burlingtons.

The original Kent design intended for the exedra at Chiswick but rejected by Burlington and later used for the Temple of British Worthies at Stowe.

When Kent first started his gardening career he was still influenced by Burlington's ideas on art and nature, which included the architectural use of nature's materials to give the effect of columns and arcades. At Holkham Kent's first design for a seat on the hill showed the Burlingtonian building set in a semicircular topiary arcade; in a later design Kent disposed of the clipped arcade to allow the building to stand freely in the landscape. At Chiswick Burlington's stone orangery with its flanking verdant keystoned effect arcade would remain; as would his straight *patte d'oie* allées terminated by his buildings, however much the pictorially minded Kent might wish to remove them.

Burlington, Kent and Thomas Coke were all three much preoccupied with the building of Holkham; they

Kent's design for the making of a water woodland garden at Chiswick. Kent transformed his painted scenes into picturesque gardening.

were on very intimate terms and enjoyed good-natured banter. In 1736 in a letter to Lord Burlington Coke reported that 'unpictoresk cold & insipid strait walks' which 'even Mr Pope himself cd not by description enliven' made 'the signor sick'.[28] Although he was not specifically referring to the earl's 'damn dull walks', there is no doubt that Burlington was meant to get Kent's message and the sly remark as to why Chiswick did not merit a mention in Pope's gardening verses in his *Epistle*.

When the remark on what the Signor found un-picturesque was made (the first recorded time that the concept of the picturesque, clearly Kent's own, was used in connection with gardening) he was working on Lord Cobham's Elysian Fields at Stowe, which Southcote saw as 'the painting part' of the gardens as opposed to the part of the gardens laid out 'in the Bridgeman taste'.[29] There was much political and moral satire in the Elysian Fields with a distinct Popeian flavour such as the pristine condition of Kent's Temple of Ancient Virtue and the Temple of Modern Virtue being in ruins with a headless statue of Sir Robert Walpole inside. On the other side of the river looking up to the classical men of virtue, recalling Pope's own 'Temple of Fame', was the Kent monument, the original design for which Burlington had rejected for the Chiswick exedra, and which was now called the Temple of British Worthies, amongst whom Pope was enshrined. A joke which Kent and Pope would have shared was the eulogy to Signor Fido on the back of the British Worthies building; he turned out to be a faithful hound.

The Elysian Fields at Stowe. 'This garden is beyond all description in the New Part of It', Pope wrote excitedly in 1739. Kent had here realised the Elysian gardening the poet had only 'imaged'.

Pope had always admired the Bridgeman layout at Stowe which he had praised in his *Epistle to the Earl of Burlington* in 1731, but on a visit in 1739 he wrote to Martha Blount, 'this Garden is beyond all description in the New Part of It; I am every hour in it, but dinner and night and every hour Envying myself the delight of it'.[30] His only regret was that Martha was not there with him to add her appreciation to his enjoyment of it, as in the early days when they shared Arcadia in Windsor Forest. In the Elysian Fields Pope saw the embodiment of the gardening ideas that he had only hinted at in the *Epistle*.

Kent pursued his ideas of abandoning the 'level and the line' by making drawings of garden scenes, rather than actual plans. Walpole said, 'the pencil of his imagi-nation bestowed all the arts of landscape on the scenes he handled. The great principles on which he worked were perspective, and light and shade'.[31] As the historian of 'modern gardening' Walpole thought, however, that Kent had taken many of his ideas of 'opening and retiring shades' in perspective planting from Pope's garden. Spence maintained that Pope and Kent were 'the first that practiced painting in gardening' which covered 'perspective, prospect, distancing and attracting'.[32] However, as Walpole understood and Pope would undoubtedly have agreed, Kent added his own ideas of picturesque gardening which went beyond the techniques of perspective, Pope had indicated when he told Spence in 1734 that 'all gardening is landscape painting'.[33]

1. Horace Walpole acquired the Vertue manuscript notebooks in 1759 and frequently quoted from them: there is much information about Kent and Lord Burlington in material published in the Walpole Society Annual Volume, vol.XXII.
2. Michael I. Wilson, *William Kent*, 1985, pp.80-85. See also *Pallas enthron'd*, catalogue to exhibition of work by Lady Burlington, Orleans House Gallery, Twickenham, 1999.
3. *The Twickenham Edition of the Poems of Alexander Pope*, ed. John Butt, X, p.390.
4. See Mavis Batey, 'Gilpin and the schoolboy Picturesque', *Garden History*, vol.2, no.2 (1974), pp.24-26. Imaging and 'painting to the mind' were synonymous. Pope greatly admired Thomas Parnell's poem 'Health, an Eclogue', 1722, in which he praises Virgil's Muse, which 'Paints rural Prospects and the Charms of Sight'
5. Mavis Batey *et al.*, *Arcadian Thames*, pp.95-96.
6. M.Roethlisberger, *Claude Lorrain*, 1951, vol.1, p.37.
7. See David Jacques, 'On the supposed Chineseness of the English Garden', *Garden History*, vol.18, no.2 (1990), pp.190-91, notes 13 and 16.
8. Spence, *Observations*, no.419.
9. Richard Hurd, *Letters on Chivalry and Romance*,1762, Letter XII, p.120.
10. William Mason. *The English Garden*, Book 1, note x, v.511.
11. *Correspondence*, 3:322-23.
12. Joseph Warton, *An Essay on the Genius and Writing of Pope*, 1782, vol.II, p.244.
13. Gilbert West, *Stowe. The Gardens of the Rt. Hn. Richard Lord Viscount Cobham*, 1732, ll.79-80.
14. See Richard Wheeler, 'The Gardens of Stowe and West Wycombe', *Apollo*, April 1977.
15. Egremont Diary, Hist. Mss Comm., vol.II, p.138.
16. *Modern Gardening*, p.270. Spence, *Observations*, no.1060. Spence indicated that Kent worked in the Bayswater area, which Rocque shows in a wild state.
17. Pope, *Imitations of Horace*, 1738, Satire II, Book II, ll.175-77.
18. *Correspondence*, 3:417.
19. *Correspondence*, 4:44.
20. Now in the National Maritime Museum at Greenwich.
21. *Modern Gardening*, p.268.
22. Hist. Mss Comm, vol.XLII, Carlisle, p.144.
23. Ibid.
24. *Modern Gardening*, p.264.
25. See Thomas Whately, *Observations on Modern Gardening*, 1801, p.153. Bridgeman's 'plegmatic planting' is compared to Kent's 'gentle unevenesses'.
26. Spence, *Observations*, no.1060.
27. John Dixon Hunt, *Garden and Grove*, 1986, pp.214-15.
28. H.Avray Tipping, 'Four unpublished Letters of William Kent', *Architectural Review*, LXIII, 1928, p.210.
29. Spence, *Observations*, no.1122.
30. *Correspondence*, 4:185.
31. *Modern Gardening*, p.264.
32. Spence, *Observations*, no.603.
33. Spence, *Observations*, no.606. Part of his pictorial idea was to look through a frame. At the time of the remark Pope was looking through the arched gateway of the Oxford Botanic Garden.

NATURE BEING IMITATED AND IMPROVED

Rousham, where Kent 'leaped the fence and saw that all nature was a Garden'. The visitor walked down to Scheemakers' dramatic statue of the lion devouring the horse at the end of the bowling green and his eye was then taken on to the Oxfordshire countryside beyond and the eyecatcher on the hill.

P OPE next advances: his indignant arm
Waves the poetic brand o'er Timon's shades,
And lights them to destruction; the fierce blaze
Sweeps thro' each kindred Vista; Groves to Groves
Nod their fraternal farewell, and expire.
And now, elate with fair-earn'd victory,
The Bard retires, and on the Bank of Thames
Erects his flag of triumph; wild it waves
In verdant splendor, and beholds, and hails
The King of Rivers, as he rolls along.
KENT is his bold associate, KENT who felt
The pencil's power: but, fir'd by higher forms
Of Beauty, than that pencil knew to paint,
Work'd with the living hues that Nature lent,
And realiz'd his Landscapes. Generous He,
Who gave to Painting, what the wayward Nymph
Refus'd her Votary, those Elysian scenes,
Which would she emulate, her nicest hand
Must all its force of light and shade employ.

William Mason, *The English Garden*, 1772, lines 500–18.

Horace Walpole, as an authoritative eyewitness, has left us a lively and revealing history of landscape gardening. He had no hesitation in claiming that it was Kent who 'invented the new style' and that 'Mr Pope undoubtedly contributed to form his taste'. Walpole was careful to give due credit for the 'reformation' to Charles Bridgeman, who had worked for his father at Houghton, detecting 'many detached thoughts' in his layouts that 'strongly indicate the dawn of modern taste'; Bridgeman's general arrangement, however, was still in the formal French style and the hand of the designer's art very apparent. William Kent went beyond 'detached thoughts' and, in Walpole's famous words, 'leaped the fence, and saw that all nature was a garden'. Walpole was in no doubt that it was Kent who was 'the inventor of an art that realizes painting and improves Nature'.[1]

Walpole's essay 'On Modern Gardening' in his fourth volume of *The Anecdotes of Painting* and William Mason's verse history in the first book of *The English Garden* are complementary. Walpole himself was a great lover of poetry and was devastated by the death of his friend Thomas Gray, whose poems he had published on his Strawberry Hill press.[2] 'Recollect I have lived with Gray and seen Pope', he once boasted in later life when poetry was being discussed.[3] After Gray's death, their mutual friend William Mason took his place as Walpole's 'confessor in literature' and also as his gardening ally. Mason, who was a great admirer of Pope, shared Walpole's idea that poetry, painting and gardening were three sister Muses.[4] In his *The English Garden* he set out to give the youngest Muse of 'modern gardening' a native origin and principles parallel to poetry and painting.

Walpole and Mason both pointed to poets, particularly Spenser and Milton, as the inspiration for landscape sensibility, and to Pope, through his pastoral poetry and his *Epistle to the Earl of Burlington*, as the true champion of landscape gardening. Having confounded the false taste of Timon's villa and pointed the way forward, Pope retired to his Twickenham retreat, according to Mason, and encouraged his 'bold associate', Kent, to carry out his ideas; thus, through Pope and Kent the desirable 'poet's feeling and painter's eye' would unite in the art of landscape gardening. A note to the text (see page opposite) explained that Kent's picturesque gardening scenes far excelled those he had conjured up in painting.[5]

When Walpole and Mason were commenting in the 1760s on the originality of Kent's Pope-inspired work, his landscapes had matured, but Burlington's friend, Sir Thomas Robinson, had recognised the same 'new taste' in 'Mr Kent's notion of gardening', thirty years before when Kent had only just set out on his career. 'When finished', Robinson wrote approvingly to the Earl of Carlisle, 'it has the appearance of beautiful nature' (see page 104). The concept of 'beautiful nature' was in the tradition of neoclassical beauty, the idealised world beyond sense perception; Plato's innate ideas which Lockean philosophy had refuted, maintaining that man came into the world with a 'blank slate'. In the notes to his *Dunciad*, Pope recalls Shaftesbury's neo-classical philosopher, Theocles, who, in his walks, invoked the 'genius of the Place' to obtain at least some faint and distant view of the *Sovereign Genius* and first *beauty*' of 'glorious Nature'.[6]

Dryden, in the Preface to his translation of Du Fresnoy's *The Art of Painting*, maintained that it was the role of the artist to, 'Correct and amend the common Nature, and to represent it as it was first created without fault'.[7] Spence saw Kent's 'beautiful nature' in the landscape garden as aiming to follow idealised Italian landscapes rather than the 'common nature of Dutch painting'.[8] This was a far cry from Burlington's 'natural taste' or Castell's 'imitatio ruris', where 'common nature' was introduced to contrast with formal gardening. It was, however, akin to Pope's 'imaging' of the 'beautiful nature' of the golden age in his Homer translations and pastoral poetry. Pope knew well, however, that landscaping needed more than poetic visions, and urged gardeners

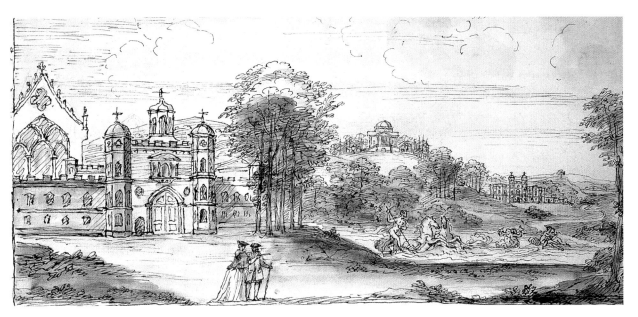

Kent's landscape capriccio for Michael Drayton's *Poly-Olbion*, celebrating the beauties of his native land. Where the Thames meets the river Mole at Hampton Court, it also celebrates Kent's own involvement with work at the Thameside palace and at Esher on the Mole.

that consulting the Genius should include considering 'the Use of the Place, and the Beauties not forced into it, but arising from it'.

Pope and Addison had decried 'artificial shows' in gardens preferring the sight of nature's forests and meadows, but Kent set out to prove that nature could be improved so that it would appear, in Robinson's words, as though 'art had no part in the finishing'. According to Mason, it was from Spenser's romantic idealism that William Kent 'caught his taste in gardening' in the natural way.[9] In the early eighteenth century there was as yet no literary attitude known as romanticism, but Kent introduced romantic ideas into his gardening in the existing sense of the word as 'resembling the tales of romance'; this was not just by making romantic hermitages and caves but in the whole idea of the unseen hand or art in the planting of a paradisal garden. Mason himself points to the lines in *The Faerie Queene* which he sees as the major tenet of such romantic landscape improvement:

For all that Nature, by her mother wit,
Could frame in earth and form of substance base

Was there; and all that Nature did omit,
Art (playing Nature's second part) supplied it.[10]

On Mason's interpretation a landscape improver should call in art 'only to second Nature and supply/All that the Nymph forgot, or left forlorn'.[11]

Nature playing at imitating her own imitative art was a compelling Renaissance idea. As well as illustrating Spenser, Kent had begun illustrating Tasso and Ariosto's works, from which Spenser had taken the idea of artful imitations of nature. In Tasso's words in his *Jerusalem Delivered*, 'Nature played a sportive part/ and strove to mock the mimic works of art'. The Bower of Bliss of Spenser's Acrasia, modelled on Tasso's Armida's enchanted garden, offered a flowery paradise with 'trembling groves' and crystal streams and in these romantic scenes 'the art, which all that wrought, appeared in no place'.[12]

The art for a Spenserian garden designer was to choose a romantic situation, 'a place pickt out by choice of best alive/that nature's worke by art can imitate' in order to allow Nature to play her sportive part in outdoing Art.[13] Clearly Samuel Boyse, a minor poet who visited Kent's grotto in the Elysian Fields at Stowe in 1742,

The grotto at Stowe was partly modelled on Pope's but placed in a more romantic situation.

William Mason's flower garden. In Nuneham's garden of romance flowers were grown 'in the natural way of gardening', but with nature imitating art.

thought that this had been achieved there, when he was inspired to write in a poem on Stowe called 'The Triumphs of Nature':

> *Where stands the lonesome grotto sweetly plac'd*
> *With all the art of sportive nature grac'd.*[14]

When Kent was given free rein in his gardening he introduced romantic naturally entwined arbours and tree draperies into garden walks and groves, such as Ariosto described in *Orlando Furioso*:

> *Small thickets, with the scented laurel gay,*
> *Cedar and orange, full of fruit and flower,*
> *Myrtle and palm, with interwoven spray*
> *Pleached in mixed modes form a bower.*[15]

It is unlikely that Kent was allowed to introduce romantic woodland arbours and 'mixed modes' of planting at Chiswick or in Bridgeman's main layout at Stowe but he seems to have done so at Esher; in Pope's words: '…in Esher's peaceful Grove/(Where *Kent* and Nature vye for *Pelham's* Love)'.[16]

Romantic effects of nature vying harmoniously with art (in this case the hand of Kent) would be particularly apposite at Esher as Kent was asked to Gothicise the house to recall its medieval past as a Wolsey residence. An illustration by Kent for *Poly-Olbion* in which, in 1598, Michael Drayton had sought to awaken his countrymen to the beauties of their native land, shows Esher and Hampton Court, where Kent had rebuilt part of the Tudor Clock Tower court, in a Thames capriccio setting (page 114). Walpole comments approvingly on the Esher grotto set into the side of the hill 'overhung to a vast height with woodbines, lilacs and laburnum and dignified by those tall shapely cypresses'; an example of 'mixed mode' picturesque planting which he particularly liked.[17]

Carlton House gardens. The gardens, laid out for Frederick, Prince of Wales, were probably Kent's first commission to design a garden rather than garden buildings. He planted flowers in a new natural way.

Spence said that Southcote had influenced Kent when the latter worked at Woburn and prevailed on him 'to resume flowers in the natural way of gardening'.[18] Southcote was a relative of Lord Petre who was an outstanding botanist-gardener.[19] Pope had always relished 'nosegays' at Twickenham and Marble Hill had its 'sweet walk'. Walpole's 'romantic inclinations' craved secluded spots at Strawberry Hill where he could enjoy Milton's blossoming 'wilderness of sweets' and the fragrance of flowers 'worthy of paradise' as well as his beloved Thames landscape views.[20] William Mason later created a romantic flower garden for their mutual friend Lord Nuneham at the entrance of which were lines from the 'Romance of the Rose' depicting the Garden of Mirth with its gay flowers making the ground 'queint and poudrid as men had it peint'.[21]

It was Kent, however, according to William Burgh's notes for Mason's *The English Garden*, who specialised in mixing flowering shrubs and evergreens, giving picturesque effect by tinting and change of texture.[22] Kent ordered a prodigious number of plants for the Prince of Wales's Carlton House garden in Pall Mall, which Sir Thomas Robinson hailed as such a successful innovation in 1734. Some 15,000 trees were supplied for the 9 acre garden including 2000 shrubs and climbers such as lilacs, honeysuckles, roses, jasmines and sweet briars; there were also hundreds of herbaceous plants and thousands of bulbs; some of these were destined for the flower garden but others were for the grove by the side of the central octagon pavilion.[23] If the flowering content was, as Spence said, influenced by Southcote, the planting effect is likely to have been very different. A plan made by Southcote shows his own shrubbery was planted in a 'theatrical' with a wide border of herbaceous plants and rows of shrubs stepped up to an original hedgerow.[24]

Left. The statues play an important part in Rousham's associative garden. Bacchus is seen here in a small secluded dell by the river (naturalised from the Bridgeman theatre). Bacchus, Ceres and Mercury were grouped round 'a very fine Fountain, that plays 40ft high and falls down among shells', according to the gardener, but the fountain is now missing.

Below. The Longhorn cattle within the ha-ha show Rousham as a ferme ornée. The manor house and the outlying farm buildings were gothicised.

At Rousham in Oxfordshire, Kent's last garden where he is seen at his best, we can envisage a wilder effect and imagine just how romantic his flowery woodlands were when nature and art were 'striving each th'other to undermine' in the Spenserian manner. John Clary, the Rousham gardener who carried out Kent's instructions, recounts with understandable pride how the unobtrusive hand of art assisted nature's works:

In one of the noblest Green Serpentine Walks, that was ever seen, or even made, view narrowly as you walk along, and youl perhaps see, a greater veriaty of evergreens, and Flowering Shrubs, then you can posably see in any one walk in the World, at the end of this walk stands a four Seat Forrist Chair, where you set down and view what, and where, you have walked a long, their you see the deferant sorts of Flowers, peeping through the deferant sorts of Evergreens, here you think the

Kent's Praeneste at Rousham can be seen on the hillside in his illustration of Phaedria's Island (see page 102). It was modelled on the Temple of Fortune at Praeneste visited on the Grand Tour.

Laurel produces a Rose, the Holly a Syringa, the Yew a Lilac, and the sweet Honeysuckle is peeping out from under every Leafe, in short they are so mixt together, that youd thing every Leafe of the Evergreens, produced one flower or a nother.[25]

At Rousham Kent was in charge of the whole garden and parkland and not just individual picturesque scenes. Pope went to see his work in 1739 after he had visited Stowe with such pleasure.[26] As he had at Stowe, Pope had also enjoyed the former Bridgeman layout at Rousham[27], but Kent was then transforming the whole garden for General Dormer, who inherited in 1737, not just laying out a new area like the Elysian Fields at Stowe which were an addition to the vast Bridgeman gardens. The general, who had been badly wounded at the Battle of Blenheim, was in failing health and spent most of his time in London where he was in touch with Burlington and Pope and his cousin and heir, Sir Clement Cottrell, who lived at Twickenham. Kent was clearly often present at the meetings on friendly terms as in 1736 Pope observed that he 'is become a happy but plumper copy' of Dormer.[28]

It was Burlington himself who arranged for Kent to plan the garden at Rousham for James Dormer's 'philosophic retirement', but the general, who died in 1741, had little time in which to enjoy it. As so many of the discussions about Kent's plans for the house and garden took place in London, the Rousham steward, William White, had to write weekly accounts to the general about progress.[29] His letters shed much light on the day to day workings of the creation of a most important, and largely unchanged, Kent landscape garden; the steward also drew up a plan of the work, which Kent did not normally undertake, so that it is possible to see how he worked over the former Bridgeman plan.[30] Kent removed the terracing down to the River Cherwell and Bridgeman's parapets alongside the riverside walk; sloped the turf down to natural banks of the slightly-widened river; he remoulded the land beyond Bridgeman's Elm Walk allée and extended it to the gothicised Heyford Bridge.

The general was a literary, cultivated man and is said to have enjoyed reading Pope's verses in his garden;[31] his chief interest was in having an associative garden for his antique sculptures.[32] Kent arranged these in a series of picturesque scenes by removing Bridgeman's bastion viewpoint and planting the garden as different episodes. The best 'management of surprises'[33] was the climax of the garden, the Spenserian Venus Vale and its rustic grotto cascade and dancing satyrs. 'Sure no Tongue can express the Beautyfull view that presents itself to your eye', wrote Clary the gardener. Halfway down an adjacent hidden wooded slope was Proserpina's cave[34] and as befitted the walk to the Underworld, the gardener, acting under Kent's instructions said his planting was as 'dark and melencholly as it was posable to make it' (but apparently Kent had by now been laughed out of planting dead trees for grisly effect). The visitor would, however, feel the strong contrast in mood compared with the delights of the flowery serpentine shrubbery that had just been left.

Following Southcote's ideas for his ferme ornée at Woburn,[35] Kent gave Rousham's visitors a perimeter walk before they came to the picturesque scenes of Venus Vale and the Praeneste Arcade from the level ground by the river (as seen in Kent's Faerie Queene illustration of Phaedria's Island, page 102). The 'roundabout walk' allowed various gothic buildings to be seen across the grazed fields as part of a rural scene. The seventeenth-century manor house was gothicised with battlements and a turret and there was also a gothic lodge, which was the public pedestrian entrance from the highway and even gothic cow byres; on the other side of the river Cuttle Mill was bepinnacled and a gothic triumphal arch erected on a distant hill to recall the general's military exploits.

The general's statues, excepting those in the concealed Venus Vale, looked out on to the Oxfordshire countryside with eyecatcher, planting and views by courtesy of the Rousham neighbours. Pope's idea of a garden scheme that 'calls in the country, catches opening glades' was achieved in a way that the writer of the Epistle could never have envisaged; his only thoughts on the matter concerned the straight ha-ha at Stowe, which extended

Bridgeman's vistas into Castell's 'imitatio ruris' (see page 82). Walpole called Kent's ha-ha, which followed the contours and united the garden and the countryside unobtrusively, a 'Kent-fence'. It was to become an essential component of a landscape garden.[36]

Although Walpole saw Rousham as the 'most engaging' of Kent's works in which he made 'the whole sweet' he was writing in the 1760s when 'Capability' Brown was transforming thousands of acres of the countryside on a scale that Kent could never have attempted. 'That Kent's ideas were but rarely great, was in some measure owing to the novelty of his art', was how Walpole saw it with hindsight: 'it would have been difficult to have transported the style of gardening at once from a few acres to tumbling of forests'.[37] James Thomson also recognised that Pope's Twickenham garden was only 'in miniature'[38], but at Rousham in the small scale Venus Vale Walpole detected the influence of Pope, 'I do not know whether the disposition of the garden…..was not planned on the model of Mr Pope's, at least in the opening and retiring shades of Venus's vales'.[39]

Kent had certainly learned much from what Walpole

called Pope's 'little perspective' garden of a few acres at Twickenham and Walpole could trace the progress of the ideas of Pope, Southcote and Kent to 'Capability' Brown's final 'tumbling of forests'. At Kent's death in 1748 Walpole lamented, 'there is a great danger everywhere of our relapsing into bad taste, for scarce any school retains its purity after the death of the institutor'.[40] It would not be long, however, before Lancelot Brown, who had worked with Kent at Stowe would set up his own practice at Hammersmith, after Kent's death, and become the good friend of Walpole and Mason.[41] In concluding his 'On Modern Gardening' Walpole said with satisfaction, 'It was fortunate for the country and Mr Kent, that he was succeeded by a very able master'.[42] When Brown died in 1783 Walpole, with due respect to both masters of the natural style, hailed him as 'Lady Nature's second husband'.[43] Pope's encouraging words 'Let Nature never be forgot' had yielded a rich harvest.

Kent's drawing of his Venus Vale at Rousham. Kent excelled in creating picturesque scenes like stage sets. His work at Rousham survives unchanged by later fashions.

1. *Anecdotes of Painting*, ed. Dallaway, p.222. For the Walpole quotes from *Modern Gardening* see text on page 106.
2. Gray's poems 'The Progress of Poetry' and 'The Bard' were the first fruits of the Strawberry Hill press in 1757.
3. Walpole, *Correspondence*, 1:310. See Patricia Astley Cooper, *Alexander Pope's Twickenham*, 1988, p.34, for suggestion of possible Walpole/Pope meeting.
4. Mason's *Satirical Poems*, with notes by Walpole, ed. Paget Toynbee, 1926, p.43.
5. Mason, *The English Garden*, Book I, ll.500-14. Walpole, *Correspondence*, 9:116. Walpole similarly condemned Kent's illustrations of *The Faerie Queene*, which he said was a 'very favourite work' of his but showed him in 'the worst possible light as an artist'.
6. *Dunciad*, Book IV, l.488, 'which Theocles to raptur'd vision saw'. Pope gives reference to Shaftesbury, *Characteristics*, vol.2, p.245.
7. *De Arte Graphica*, 1695, preface p.v.
8. Spence, *Observations*, no. 1069.
9. Mason, *The English Garden*, Book I, note x to l.511.
10. Spenser, *The Faerie Queene*, Book IV, Canto II; the passage immediately alluded to is in the 21st stanza.
11. Mason, *The English Garden*, Book I, l.445.
12. *The Faerie Queene*, Book II, Canto XII.
13. Ibid.
14. Samuel Boyse, 'The Triumphs of Nature', *Descriptions of Lord Cobham's Gardens at Stowe 1700-50*, ed. G.B.Clarke, ll.274-75.
15. As translated in Mason's Temple of Flora at Nuneham.
16. Pope, *Epilogue to the Satires*, Dialogue II, ll.66-67.
17. Walpole, *Correspondence*, 10: 73.
18. Spence, *Observations*, no.1128.
19. G.Clutton and C.Mackay, 'Old Thorndon Hall, Essex', Garden History Society Occasional Paper, no.2, 1970, pp.27-40.
20. *Arcadian Thames*, p.60.
21. See Mavis Batey, 'Nuneham Park: Romantic Vision in a Flower Garden', *Country Life*, 12 Sept. 1968.
22. Mason, *The English Garden*, Book I, note II to verse 395.

23. David Coombs, 'The Garden at Carlton House', *Garden History*, vol.25, no.2 (1997), pp.153-77.
24. Plan shown in *Garden History*, vol.2, no.3 (1974), p.40. For the origins of 'theatrical planting', see Mark Laird: *The Flowering of the Landscape Garden*, 1999, ch.1.
25. Mavis Batey, 'The Way to View Rousham by Kent's Gardener', *Garden History*, vol.11, no.2, (1983), p.129.
26. *Correspondence*, 4:188.
27. *Correspondence*, 2:53.
28. *Correspondence*, 4:43.
29. Ulrich Müller, 'Rousham: A Transcription of the Steward's Letters', *Garden History*, vol.25, no.2 (1997), pp.178-88.
30. Unsigned plan in Bodleian Library, Oxford, Ms Gough Drawings a.4.f.63, attributed to Bridgeman.
31. His library sale after his death took twenty days with over 3000 lots, mainly of classical and French literature. Horace Walpole was a buyer. 'Rowshamius Hortus', an anonymous Latin poem, published in *The Museum: or the Literary and Historical Register*, 3, XXXII, 1747, included the lines: 'Hic Scipio solitus vestigia tendere, carmen/Arrecta Popii suaviloquum aure bibens'.
32. For a schedule of the sculptures acquired by Kent's 'bronzomad general', see Hal Moggridge, HBMC Report (1982), reprinted in the *Journal of Garden History*, vol.6, p.241.
33. Spence, *Observations*, no:612.
34. For Proserpina see David Coffin, 'The Elysian Fields of Rousham', *Proceedings of the American Philosophical Society*, vol.130, no.4, 1986, p.412.
35. See R.W.King, 'Philip Southcote and Woburn Farm', *Garden History*, vol.2, no.3 (1974), pp.27-60.
36. Walpole, *Correspondence*, 9:88.
37. *Modern Gardening*, 268-69.
38. James Thomson, 'Liberty', v.698.
39. Walpole, *Modern Gardening*, p.268-69
40. Walpole, *Correspondence*, 30: 114.
41. *Arcadian Thames*, p.34.
42. Walpole, *Modern Gardening*, p.280.
43. Walpole, *Correspondence*, 33: 385.

$\mathcal{E}PILOGUE$

The engraving of Turner's *View of Pope's Villa at Twickenham
during its Dilapidations*. Turner greatly admired Pope
and was deeply moved when he witnessed the
destruction of his villa in 1807.

*S*LOW *let us trace the matchless Vale of Thames;*
Fair-winding up to where the Muses haunt
In Twitnam's bowers, and for their Pope implore
The healing God; to royal Hampton's pile,
To Clermont's terraced height, and Esher's groves,
Where in the sweetest solitude, embraced
By the soft windings of the silent Mole,
From courts and senates Pelham finds repose
Enchanting vale! Beyond whate'er the Muse
Has of Achaia or Hesperia sung!
O vale of bliss! O softly-swelling hills!
On which the Power of Cultivation lies,
And joys to see the wonders of his toil.

    Heavens! What a goodly prospect spreads around,
Of hills, and dales, and woods, and lawns, and spires,
And glittering towns, and gilded streams, till all
The stretching landscape into smoke decays!

James Thomson, *The Seasons: Summer*, 1744 (written as Pope lay dying).

TWICKENHAM BECAME A SHRINE AS THE 'HAUNT of the Muses' after Pope's death in 1744. Robert Dodsley had the previous year already published a collection of verse on Pope's garden and grotto and this was reprinted in John Serle's 1745 guidebook. In 1747 William Mason portrayed Pope dying in his grotto in his poem 'Musaeus: A Monody to the Memory of Mr Pope', with the shades of Chaucer, Spenser and Milton in attendance; the Sicilian Muse of pastoral poetry leads her weeping sister Muses to the solemn scene; shepherds have forsaken their flocks and the Thames sighs as it flows by the 'widow'd grot'. The grotto, an epitome of Pope's life, which still survives today, became an icon to the poet and his way of life.

Pope had been dead for three years when Walpole settled at Strawberry Hill, but he said that his neighbour's ghost skimmed by his windows in 'poetic moonlight'.[1] It is remarkable that two such major figures as Pope and Walpole should have chosen the same locality. They had settled by the rural Thames away from pomp and formality, where they could realise their own visions – classical Arcadia for Pope and the romance of the Middle Ages for Walpole.

Walpole greatly admired Pope and acquired the pocket copy of Homer's *Iliad* that the poet used for translation to put on display in his library. His own little gothic castle owed much to the climate of sensibility that Pope had inspired, particularly to his *Eloisa to Abelard* with its Miltonic landscape of gothic cells and twilight groves. Strawberry Hill was the first neo-gothic building to be properly inhabited as opposed to the folly garden buildings such as Pope's Alfred's Hall at Cirencester or Kent's caves and hermitages. It had a Paraclete cloister so named after Eloisa's convent. Taste was undoubtedly the hallmark of Burlington's Chiswick villa, but Walpole declared that it was passion that was needed 'to feel gothic';[2] Walpole's feel for gothic was antiquarian as well as literary.

Walpole, an admirer of William Gilpin, was a patron of Picturesque tours, and Boydell's *History of the River Thames*, published in 1795 with text by William Combe, was dedicated to him. Combe described how his feelings, as a Thames tourist, were aroused as he approached the 'classic spot' where Pope 'closed a life which is the boast of his country' and then passed the riverside church 'where he was laid to rest'. Farington's illustration of Pope's villa shows it embowered in weeping willows, which the new owner, Welbore Ellis, had taken great care to preserve; one writer observed in 1789 that from one, said to have been planted by Pope himself, thousands of slips were taken away every year all over the world, even to Russia, where Catherine the Great, a great admirer of English landscape gardening, wanted some for her own garden at St Petersburg.[3]

In Walpole's lifetime his guests were taken over to see Pope's grotto, and after the great Strawberry Hill sale by Earl Waldegrave in 1842 visitors flocked over to the grotto where enterprising modern day nymphs had set up to sell shellfuls of water from the sacred spring; slips were also sold from a decayed willow stump brought into the grotto, which remains today.[4] Dodsley's prophecy in his 'Cave of Pope' had by then come true and many of the materials listed by Serle in his guide had been pilfered as souvenirs.

Then some small Gem, or Moss, or Shining Ore,
Departing, each shall filter, in fond hope
To please their Friends, on every distant Shore
Boasting a Relick from the Cave of Pope.

The villa itself had been destroyed in 1807 by the occupant, Baroness Howe, who was inconvenienced by persistent visitors anxious to see the garden and grotto; she earned the name the 'Queen of the Goths' thereby. The act of destruction was watched by J.M.W.Turner, who had just bought a plot of land for a house in Twickenham. He wrote a verse to Pope, 'to an admiring country once revered', as he watched while 'desolation hovers o'er these walls' and tried to rescue the weeping willow:

> Now to destruction doom'd thy peaceful grott
> Pope's willow bending to the earth forgot
> Save one weak scion by my fostering care
> Nursed to life.[5]

Baroness Howe did not in fact destroy the grotto along with the villa as she still needed access through the tunnel to the garden across the road; the entrance arch of the grotto then appeared as free standing when seen from the river.

Turner feelingly painted an elegiac view of *Pope's Villa at Twickenham during its Dilapidation*, which showed workmen with relics from the poet's house in the midst of a pastoral scene (page 124). John Landseer, reviewing the painting when it was exhibited in Turner's gallery in 1808 wrote, 'At the sight of this picture who but will be induced to pause, and reflect on the celebrity and the superlative merits of Pope? Who but will recollect that the landscape which has caught the eye and called forth the talents of Turner, has resounded to his lyre?' Landseer felt strongly that the painting should be seen by a wider audience and it was in fact the first time that Turner became aware of the potential of line engraving for this purpose and used the medium to promote Pope's memorial through John Britton's publication, *Fine Arts of the English School*.[6]

Turner's homage to Pope in poetry and painting was personal as well as national in feeling. He devoted much time to his 'Verse Book', which was greatly influenced by Pope and Thomson, who were his inspiration for poetic landscape. He felt a strong bond with Pope's Virgilian evocation of Arcadia on the Thames, calling him 'the British Maro'. He used to read Pope's translations of Homer as he was rowed along the river, conjuring up classical scenes, which must have contributed largely to his decision to settle in Twickenham. Ruskin regretted that Turner should see fit to perpetuate the myth of Arcadian rural felicity, which he dubbed 'Twickenham classicism'.[7]

'Twickenham classicism' was no mere nostalgia for a golden age for Turner who would take Pope's poetic 'imagings' of Arcadian landscape on into the romantic imagination. Romantic had now changed in meaning from Spenserian fancy to an individual experience where the roles of the imagination and feeling were of paramount importance. The intervening cult of the Picturesque of the 1780s and 1790s had seen the visual take precedence over the literary response to landscape.[8] Turner's genius, which combined 'poet's feeling' and 'painter's eye' far transcended Picturesque theory and responded to romantic ideas of imagination, historical association and a sense of place.

Turner admired his friend Samuel Rogers's poetry and chose to illustrate his 'The Pleasures of Memory', first written in 1792. His attachment would have been strengthened by hearing that, through his admiration of Pope, Rogers had contemplated purchasing his villa at one stage but thought its associations would command

William Mason's 'Musaeus: A Monody to the memory of Mr Pope', portrays the poet dying in his grotto with the Muse of pastoral poetry leading her weeping sisters to the solemn scene. The grotto, which still survives, became an icon to Pope.

Joseph Farington's illustration of Pope's Villa for Boydell's *History of the River Thames*, 1794. Thames tourists revered Twickenham as the 'haunt of the Muses' as they passed his villa embowered in the willows he planted and the riverside church where he was buried.

too high a price.⁹ In the Preface to his poem Rogers associated the Pleasures of Memory with the 'love of country' and the emotion of 'celebrated scenes' which 'addresses our finer feelings'. He pointed to 'the charm historic scenes impart' in the romantic imagination:

What softened views thy magic glass reveals,
When o'er the landscape Time's meek twilight steals.

'Memory sweet' was an abiding influence in Turner's life and art. He wanted to have 'Thank Time for all his Jewels' as his epitaph.¹⁰

When Turner settled into the 'matchless Vale of Thames' which had been home to Thomson and Pope he brought a new sensibility to landscape through a romantic sense of place. The two Augustan poets were ever present in the creative processes of Turner's mind at this time and he left in his Verse Book the draft of a long poem in imitation of Thomson's *The Seasons* which was inextricably linked with Pope; one section was devoted to an 'Invocation of Thames to 'The Seasons' upon the demolition of Pope's House'.¹¹ At the same time he combined ideal and real scenes in his 1809 painting of *Thomson's Aeolian Harp* in which he distorted the view to show Thomson's view from Richmond Hill, Pope's Twickenham and his own Sandycombe Lodge in the making. Claude's mythological landscape and Pope's Arcadian Thames had fused in Turner's romantic history painting.

When he exhibited the painting in his Gallery in 1809 Turner attached thirty-two completed lines from his lyrical poem which brought the legacy of Pope and Thomson together:

> *On Thomson's tomb the dewy drops distil,*
> *Soft tears of pity shed for Pope's lost fane.*
> *To worth and verse adheres sad memory still,*
> *Scorning to wear ensnaring fashion's chain.*

In the left hand corner of Turner's painting can be seen Alexis seeking the shade, with whom Alexander Pope identifies in his 'Summer' pastoral. 'A Shepherd's Boy (he seeks no better name)/Let forth his Flocks along the silver Thame'. Turner laments for Pope as Alexis:

> *In silence go fair Thames for all is laid;*
> *His pastoral reeds united and harp unstrung,*
> *Sunk is their harmony in Twickenham's glade.*
> *While flows thy stream, unheed'd and unsung.* [12]

From the same viewpoint Thomson inserted these additional lines in the 1744 edition of *The Seasons*, when Pope lay dying:

> *Slow let us trace the matchless Vale of Thames;*
> *Fair-winding up to where the Muses haunt*
> *In Twitnam's bowers, and for their Pope implore*
> *The healing God.*[13]

Thomson's full description of the 'matchless vale' from his poem was attached to a tree on Richmond Hill,

J.M.W.Turner, *Thomson's Aeolian Harp*, 1809. Turner sheds 'soft tears of pity' for Pope, who is depicted as Alexis, the Virgilian shepherd boy of his Summer pastoral, in the left-hand corner of the picture.

which became a place of pilgrimage. In 1782 Goethe's romantic friend, Pastor Moritz, was overcome by the hallowed view, which Turner was to immortalise in his paintings:[14]

whatever is charming in nature, or pleasing in art is to be seen here. Nothing I had ever seen is to be compared to it. My feelings, during the few, short, enraptured minutes that I stood there, it is impossible for any pen to describe....Here it was that Thomson and Pope gleaned from nature all those beautiful passages, with which their inimitable writings abound.[15]

Pope's sensibility to landscape through imaging, classical reveries, living in tune with nature, and a sense of place had not lost its relevance and inspiration even in a more romantic age. The influence of Pope and Thomson was still felt over a century later when there was a threat of development at Marble Hill which would have despoiled the famous view of 'Twitnam's bowers' from Richmond Hill. 'Indignation' meetings were held which led, in 1902, to the first Act of Parliament to save a view. Prominent on the Richmond Committee was the Kyrle Society, founded by Octavia and Miranda Hill in 1876 to acquire and enhance open spaces for public benefit and so-named in memory of the benefactor John Kyrle, who gave the citizens of Ross a viewpoint over the river Wye and earned Pope's praise. The Thames Landscape Strategy, launched by the Minister of the Environment in 1994, is a pioneering attempt to conserve and enhance the cultural identity of the river from Kew to Hampton, the cradle of landscape gardening, by adapting all to Pope's 'Genius and Use of the Place'.[16]

1.   Walpole, *Correspondence*, 37:270.
2.   See Kenneth Clark, *The Gothic Revival*, 1962, chapter 3.
3.   S. Felton, *Gleanings on Gardens*, 1897, p.99, extract from *The Topographer*, 1789.
4.   See *Gentleman's Magazine*, July 1842.
5.   Turner's 'Verse Book', p.11. Transcriptions of Turner's 'Verse Book' by Rosalind Mallord Turner are to be found in Andrew Wilton, *Painting and Poetry*, catalogue for Turner exhibition, Tate Gallery, 1990.
6.   See Luke Hermann, 'John Landseer on Turner', *Turner Studies*, vol.7, no.1.
7.   John Ruskin, *Works*, ed. E.T.Cook and A.Wedderburn, 1903, vol.12:373.
8.   See Mavis Batey, 'The Picturesque: An Overview', *Garden History*, vol.22, no.2 (1994), pp.121-32.
9.   The Table Talk of Samuel Rogers, ed. M.Bishop, 1952, p.14.
10. Turner's Spithead sketchbook, 1807, inside front cover. See note 5.
11. Turner's Greenwich Sketchbook, 1808-9, f.11.
12. Turner's Plymouth: Hamoaze sketchbook, 1811, f.189.
13. Thomson arrived in London from Scotland in 1725 and took long walks along the Thames, particularly enjoying the view from Richmond Hill, which he described briefly in 'Summer' in *The Seasons*, 1727. After he went to live in Richmond in 1736 he added a more detailed description for the final edition in 1744. Turner acquired land in Twickenham in 1807 and built Sandycombe Lodge.
14. Turner's most famous view, now in the Tate Gallery, was *Richmond Hill, on the Prince Regent's Birthday* (1819). Joshua Reynolds, who lived at Wick House on Richmond Hill also painted a view of the Thames from the hill, his only pure landscape painting.
15. C.P.Moritz, 'Travels in 1782', in W.Mavor, *The British Tourists*, 1789-1810, vol.IV, p.61.
16. Mavis Batey *et al.*, *Arcadian Thames*, p.15. The full report by Kim Wilkie is obtainable through the Thames Landscape Strategy Co-ordinator, Holly Lodge, Richmond Park, London TW10 5HS.

BIBLIOGRAPHY

Addison, Joseph, 'The Pleasures of the Imagination', *The Spectator*, nos 411-21, 1712.

Astley Cooper, Patricia, *Alexander Pope's Twickenham*, 1988.

Batey, M., Buttery, H., Lambert, D., and Wilkie, K., *Arcadian Thames*, 1994.

Batey, Mavis, 'The Magdalen Meadows and the Pleasures of the Imagination', *Garden History*, vol.9, no.2 (1981), pp.110-17.

Batey, Mavis, 'The Way to View Rousham by Kent's Gardener', *Garden History*, vol.11, no.2 (1983), pp.125-32

Batey, Mavis, and Lambert, David, *The English Garden Tour*, 1990.

Beckles Willson, Anthony, *Alexander Pope's Grotto in Twickenham*, 1998 (first published in *Garden History*, vol.26, no.1 (1998).

Beckles Willson, Anthony, *Mr Pope and Others*, 1996.

Bradley, Richard, *General Treatise of Husbandry and Gardening*, 1726.

Brownell, Morris, *Alexander Pope and the Arts of Georgian England*, 1978.

Brownell, Morris, *Alexander Pope's Villa*, catalogue of exhibition at Marble Hill, 1980.

Carré, Jacques, 'Lord Burlington's Garden at Chiswick', *Garden History*, vol.1, no.3 (1973), pp.23-30.

Castell, Robert, *The Villas of the Ancients Illustrated*, 1728.

Clark, H.F., 'Eighteenth-century Elysiums: The Role of Association in the Landscape Movement', *Journal of the Warburg and Courtauld Institues*, 6 (1943), pp.165-89.

Clarke, George, 'Grecian Taste and Gothic Virtue: Lord Cobham's Gardening Programme and its Iconography', *Apollo*, 97 (June 1973), pp.566-71.

Coffin, David, 'The Elysian Fields of Rousham', *Proceedings of the American Philosophical Society*, vol.130, no.4 (1986).

Desmond, Ray, *Blest Retreats*, 1984.

Erskine-Hill, Howard, *The Social Milieu of Alexander Pope*, 1975.

Gilpin, William, *A Dialogue upon the Gardens of the Right Honourable the Lord Viscount Cobham at Stow in Buckinghamshire*, 1748.

Harris, John, *The Palladian Revival, Lord Burlington, His Villa and Garden at Chiswick*, 1994.

Hunt, John Dixon, and Willis, Peter, eds, *The Genius of the Place, The English Landscape Garden, 1620-1820*, 1975.

Hunt, John Dixon, *Garden and Grove, The Italian Renaissance Garden in the English Imagination: 1600-1750*, 1986.

Hunt, John Dixon, *William Kent: Landscape Garden Designer*, 1987.

Jacques, David, *Georgian Gardens*, 1983.

Jacques, David, 'The Art and Sense of the Scribblerus Club in England, 1715-35', *Garden History*, vol.4, no.1 (1976), pp. 30-53.

Johnson, Samuel, *The Lives of the English Poets*, ed. G.B.Hill, 1905.

Laird, Mark, *The Flowering of the Landscape Garden*, 1999.

Langley, Batty, *New Principles of Gardening*, 1728.

Lees Milne, James, *The Earls of Creation*, 1962.

Mack, Maynard, *The Garden and the City*, 1969.

Martin, Peter, *Pursuing Innocent Pleasures, the Gardening World of Alexander Pope*, 1975.

Mason, William, *The English Garden*, 1772-81. Collected edition with William Burgh's commentary and notes, 1783.

Morris, Robert, *Defence of Ancient Architecture*, 1728.

Müller, Ulrich, 'Rousham: A Transcription of the Steward's Letters, 1738-42', *Garden History*, vol.25, no.2 (1997), pp.178-88.

Pope, Alexander, *The Correspondence of Alexander Pope*, 5 vols, ed. George Sherburn, 1956.

Pope, Alexander, *The Twickenham Edition of the Poems of Alexander Pope*, 10 vols, general editor, John Butt, 1938-61.

Sambrook, James, 'Pope and the Visual Arts', in *Writers and their Backgrounds: Alexander Pope*, ed. P.Dixon, 1972.

Serle, John, *A Plan of Mr. Pope's Garden*, 1745.

Shaftesbury, Anthony Ashley Cooper, 3rd Earl of, *Characteristicks of Men, Manners, Opinions, Times*, 1711.

Sherburn, George, *The Early Career of Alexander Pope*, 1934.

Spence, Joseph, *An Essay on Pope's Odyssey*, 1727.

Spence, Joseph, *Letters from the Grand Tour*, ed. Slava Klima, 1975.

Spence, Joseph, *Observations, Anecdotes, and Characters of Books and Men*, ed. J.M.Osborn, 2 vols, 1966.

Switzer, Stephen, *Ichnographia Rustica*, 1718.

Thacker, Christopher, *The Genius of Gardening*, 1994.

Thomson, James, *The Seasons*, 1744 edition.

Walpole, Horace, 'On Modern Gardening' in *Anecdotes of Painting*, ed. Dallaway, 1827.

Walpole, Horace, *The Correspondence of Horace Walpole*, ed. W.S.Lewis, 1937-83.

Warton, Joseph, *Essay on the Writings and Genius of Pope*, 1756.

West, Gilbert, *Stowe*, 1732, in *Descriptions of Lord Cobham's Garden at Stowe, 1700-1759*, ed. G.B.Clarke, 1990.

Willis, Peter, *Charles Bridgeman and the English Landscape Garden*, 19//.

Willis, Peter, 'Jacque Rigaud's Drawings of Stowe in the Metropolitan Museum of Art', *Eighteenth Century Studies*, vol.6, no.1 (Jan. 1972), pp.85-98.

Willis, Peter, ed., *Furor Hortensis: Essays on the History of the English Landscape Garden in Memory of H.F.Clark*, 1974.

Wilson, Michael, *William Kent*, 1985.

Wilton, Andrew, *Painting and Poetry*, catalogue for Turner exhibition, Tate Gallery, 1990 (contains Turner's 'Verse Book').

Wimsatt, William, *The Portraits of Alexander Pope*, 1965.

Woodbridge, Kenneth, 'William Kent as a Landscape Gardener: A Re-Appraisal', *Apollo*, 100 (1974).

INDEX

ACKNOWLEDGEMENTS

Special thanks to Tony Beckles Willson for all his help in many ways; also to Marco Battaggio, Jane Baxter, Robina Beckles Willson, Jeremy Benson, Julius Bryant, Margot Butt, Dick Cashmore, George Clarke, Ray Desmond, Ted Fawcett, Peter Goodchild, John Harris, the late Gemma Hunter, David Jacques, David Lambert, Lorna McRobie, Peter Martin, the late Bob Savage, the late Eileen Stamers-Smith, Michael Symes, Anthea Taigel, Kim Wilkie and, as always, my husband.

The publishers would like to add their thanks to Tony Beckles Willson and also to John Blackmore, Douglas Chambers, David Coombs, Ben Crawley, John Crawley, Jane Cunningham, Mark Davis, Peter Goodchild, Geoffrey Green, Frances Harris, Adrian Hatherall, Cathy Houghton, Marylla Hunt, Adrian James, Alun Jones, Jack Meadows, Charles Noble, Michael Symes, Patrick Taylor and Jan Woudstra.